**W9-AYR-440**

↓

free from library

# Schlepping

## Through the Alps

# Schlepping
## Through the Alps

My Search for Austria's
Jewish Past with Its Last
Wandering Shepherd

## Sam Apple

 BALLANTINE BOOKS | NEW YORK

Published in the United States by Ballantine Books, an imprint of The Random House Publishing Group, a division of Random House, Inc., New York.

Ballantine and colophon are registered trademarks of Random House, Inc.

Grateful acknowledgment is made to Magnes Press for permission to reprint translations for "S'tut Vey" and "Avreml der Marvicher" from *Anthology of Yiddish Folk Songs* Vol. 5, Hebrew University of Jerusalem, 2000.

Photograph on page 91 is reprinted courtesy of Hans Breuer.

Library of Congress Cataloging-in-Publication Data is available from the publisher upon request.

ISBN 0-345-46503-2

Printed in the United States of America

Ballantine Books website address: www.ballantinebooks.com

9 8 7 6 5 4 3 2 1

First Edition

*Text design by Barbara Sturman*

For my father

# Schlepping

## Through the Alps

# One

# A Shepherd Comes
# to Manhattan

If you're traveling the Alps with a Yiddish folksinger who also happens to be the last wandering shepherd in Austria and he assigns you the task of walking behind his flock of 625 sheep, you'll discover that the little lambs sometimes tire out and plop down for naps. Since your job is to make sure no sheep is left behind, you'll approach the sleeping lambs, your shepherd's stick firm in your right fist, and shout, *"Hop! Hop!"* You'll have learned to make this noise, which rhymes with "nope," from observing the shepherd and his sons. On occasion, when a lamb is in a deep sleep and not responding, you'll look around quickly to see whether the coast is clear. If the shepherd is far ahead or busy singing Yiddish ditties to himself, you'll kneel down next to the sleeping lamb and say, "Come on, little cutie. Time to move on." Then you'll attempt to give the lamb a quick pat on the head. Usually the lamb will wake up before you touch it and scurry ahead in search of its mother. When this happens, you'll let out several angry *hop hops*, as though you're completely in charge.

After a while on the job, you'll grow a little cocky. You'll continue along even when a few sheep are still lingering behind because you'll have learned that, for the most part, the sheep don't want to be left alone. As you walk, you'll wonder about this instinctual urge to stay close to the flock, and before you know it, you'll be lost in thoughts about evolution. You'll remember that we once traveled open landscapes in groups not unlike these sheep. You'll think about what it would be like if the sheep were forced to live apart from one another in miniature suburban homes. Would they ever find happiness? Would they greet one another while grazing in their front yards?

Suddenly, you'll reach a narrow passage and find you've drifted too far ahead and are now stuck in the middle of 625 tightly packed sheep. You'll realize that the sheep, for all their virtues, don't have much regard for human shins or feet. They'll bump their woolly sides against you from every angle until you almost lose your balance. You'll try to clear some space with your stick, but it will be no use. The sheep will treat you like the novice you are. Then, just as you're regaining your bearings, a mangy gray sheepdog will race by and bark its angry orders. Your heart will skip a beat, and you'll hurry ahead as fast as the others. If only for that one fleeting moment, you will understand the hardships of life in the flock.

After this unsettling experience, you'll remain in back.

Watching the sheep from behind, you'll note the way their ears flop when they run, turning their heads into full-bodied birds in flight; the way sheep, in the hunched position they assume to urinate, resemble kangaroos; the way even a castrated male will mount an unsuspecting ewe; the way the ewe will continue her furious nibbling at the earth as she shakes off the pesky eunuch; the way a sheep's stomach gradually expands as the day goes on, so that by sundown a cantaloupe-sized bulge has formed on its left side.

If you're on a particularly good patch of land, meaning the grass is plentiful and not too tall (sheep prefer their grass fresh), the sheep will spend a long time in one place. This is when you'll put down your backpack and look around at the snowcapped peaks and the endless expanse of Alpine foothills, hills so green and peaceful that whenever you cross them, you have to fight the desire to get down on your side and roll. You'll turn to the quiet streams cutting this way and that, pick the red flowers that peek out of crevices in the rocks, and think, *Hmm, maybe I've made a horrible mistake by overlooking a career in shepherding.*

But eventually your eyes will wander downward, and then all you'll see is shit. Sheep shit, you'll come to appreciate, is formless, unaesthetic shit; shit that, if not for the smell, could pass for mud. Next to the charming pebbles of goats or the healthy round cakes of cattle, the mushy green-brown splotches sheep leave behind can only disappoint. Still, you'll keep staring at the shit because it'll be everywhere, a parade of digested grass and Alpine flowers. You'll see one sheep's shit stacked upon another's. You'll see globs of dried shit clinging like black icicles to the wool of sheep tails. You'll get to know the shit so well that, for the first time in your life, shit will seem harmless. You'll walk through it as though you've been walking through it for years. You'll stab at it with your shepherd's stick for sport.

But a moment later you'll look down at your stick to make sure it's not too dirty because you'll have grown emotionally attached to it. You'll realize that the stick is not just a prop, but an integral part of what makes a shepherd a shepherd. You'll be so fond of your knobby wooden staff that after a while you'll accept its phallic symbolism even though you hate that sort of insight. You'll think, *The stick is my manhood. I am the stick.*

At least that's what you'll think if you're like me. But let's hope you're not like me, since then you'd also be a little too skinny. And your hair would be rather poofy. And, at age twenty-five, the only thing you'd have been really sure of was your desire to write about a singing Austrian shepherd named Hans Breuer.

I first met Hans in New York in July of 2000. A friend had forwarded me an e-mail announcement from a small Yiddish cultural outfit called Yugntruf (Call to Youth), which was sponsoring a concert and slide show by Hans at New York University. The e-mail included the following background information on Hans:

> Hans truly is a wandering Jew, for he has no permanent home. And everywhere, everywhere—Hans sings Yiddish *lidlekh* [songs] to his sheep as he leads them through valleys and over mountains. And as he goes, he thinks out loud to the sheep, and to whomever will listen, about history, politics, geography,

geology, and about being a Jew among "unknowing" racists. A peripatetic philosopher and a fine one, is Hans.

Since it's not every day I have the opportunity to meet a fine peripatetic philosopher, let alone one who sings, shows slides of his sheep, and lectures on racism, I immediately e-mailed my RSVP for the concert.

The performance space at NYU turned out to be a classroom with a wall-to-wall blackboard and about fifty desks, half of which were filled with middle-aged Jews. I took a front-row seat along with the friend who had forwarded me the e-mail.

I had expected Hans to be an old man. I imagined him with missing teeth, his back bent from years of hard labor. When Hans showed up a few minutes late, his back was straight, and his teeth, though a bit crooked, appeared to all be in place. At forty-five he was well built, husky without being heavy. He wore a black leather cap, a light pink T-shirt, sandals over his socks, and hexagonal glasses. His tangled hair, a lifeless brown, reached almost to his shoulders. Long and unruly sideburns framed his face, which struck me as vaguely Semitic, save for his strong cheekbones. After making a subtle turn to the right, his nose ended at a broad, rounded tip.

As promised, Hans had brought slides of his sheep with him. While a bushy-haired teenager fiddled with the projector, Hans addressed the audience in English, speaking slowly in an accent that brought to mind a slightly mad German professor. Due to the chaos of his travels, Hans explained, his hands moving in tandem with his words, the sheep slides had been mixed up and would not be coordinated with his songs. Although it's unlikely that anyone else in the room would have noticed the difference, Hans seemed rather upset about this technical glitch and apologized for it several more times in the course of the evening. He also apologized for not having brought his shepherd's hat. ("Normally I like very much to wear my hat when I seeng.")

When the slides were ready, Hans nodded at the young man in charge of the projector and then belted out his first song, "Hey, Tsigelech," or "Hey, Little Goats." The "hey" was held for a long note, followed by an even longer, echoing *"tsi-ge-lech."* At the time I didn't understand the words, but Hans's emotion-filled voice and intense eyes had a powerful effect. Even as I smiled at the strangeness of this gruff-looking man passionately taking on the high notes of folk ditties, there was no escaping the pull of his performance.

When Hans finished the song, he picked up a piece of paper and read the following aloud:

> "At an auction, three thousand schilling more are offered for a young cow that has been raised in the mountains—with the same milk output—than for one that has been raised down in the valley. What is the reason? It is because she is healthier. She has the Alpine herbs in her flesh and the waterfall in her blood, the air and the wind of the high mountains under her skin and the soft glowing colors of the rocks in her eyes."

I had absolutely no idea what he was talking about.

As the evening wore on, Hans mixed up the routine, performing classic Yiddish folk tunes about life in the shtetl along with hits from Yiddish musicals of the 1920s and '30s. Even during the livelier songs, which occasionally had the audience clapping along, a sense of longing resonated in Hans's voice. As he sang, he looked out over the heads of the audience and pleaded with open hands. His feet remained planted in one spot, but his upper body swayed reedlike from right to left. He might as well have been auditioning for the lead in *Fiddler on the Roof.*

Hans's melancholy demeanor made me feel all the more awful about the giggling fit that finally overtook my friend and me. Moved as I was by the pathos of Hans's voice, the slides of ewes giving birth in the background as Hans sang Yiddish show tunes was more than I could handle. I tried biting my lips, but every time I regained control, my companion's hiccups of laughter would unsettle me again. This was especially embarrassing in that I had already introduced myself to the organizers of the event as a journalist and requested an interview with Hans after the program.

Hans appeared unbothered by the laughter, and the show continued with a young woman singing several duets with him. After each song Hans stopped to read more esoteric reflections on life in the Alps. Following a song about a peasant woman pondering the ideal husband—a shoemaker? a tailor? a student?—Hans offered this:

> "What we are told not to do as children is quite normal up here [in the mountains]. You should do it here, to shout as loud as you can. . . . Shout down more than one thousand feet to your animals, driving them back from the wrong way where they move."

Hans stopped to demonstrate, startling the audience with a room-shaking bellow.

After the concert the organizers hurried Hans off, but not before he agreed to meet me for an interview the next day in Brooklyn, where he was staying at the home of a Yugntruf member. I was hoping to publish a newspaper article on Hans, but I figured that even if I couldn't, I wanted to hang out with him.

I arrived at the two-story house on a wide tree-lined street a little after 10:00 A.M. Hans answered the door and led me into a sunlit living room. He was barefoot, in a loose-fitting white T-shirt that exposed the upper reaches of his chest hair. His sagging blue work pants could have passed for cool in some circles. Now without his glasses, his long unkempt hair gave him the aura of an aging '70s rock star.

I took a seat on the couch. Hans sat down across from me, then leaned over the coffee table between us and began arranging the loose pages of a photocopied booklet. The booklet was supposed to have been handed out at the concert the night before, but Hans hadn't had enough time to put it together. It included the reflections Hans had recited between songs as well as twenty-two questions and answers about Hans's life as a wandering shepherd:

> *Question #1:* How many sheep have you got?
> *Answer:* 675 on October 6, 1997. The number changes constantly. You may ask the shepherd, then he will ask his wife and she may ask her shepherd's diary—if she finds it. . . . Or we can ask the two boys who gave the wormpowder the last time and made marks to count.

There was no small talk. I asked Hans about his background, and he began a two-hour narrative, again and again straying from his own story to talk about Austrian politics and history. His face glum, his hands struggling to convey meaning when he couldn't find the appropriate English words, Hans spoke more openly than anyone I had ever interviewed. I learned again that one should never make assumptions about this shepherd. I had assumed that he had grown up in the countryside. In fact, Hans was from Vienna. I had assumed his Jewish parents had instilled a love of Yiddish in him. In fact, only his father was Jewish, and he had taught Hans that Yiddish was a bad dialect of German. When Hans told me that his father was Jewish, I assumed his father had undergone a harrowing ordeal at the hands of the Nazis. In fact, Hans's father spent the war in England, while his non-Jewish mother, a member of the Communist resistance, was captured and tortured by the Gestapo. I had assumed that Hans had grown up in his parents' home. In fact, Hans left home for good shortly after his fifteenth birthday.

With the interview winding down, I began to feel panicked. I had great material, but I hadn't yet gotten to the bottom of the story. I still had no real understanding of why Hans was a shepherd or what Yiddish music had to do with anything in his life. Then Ilene, the owner of the house, whom I had met briefly after the concert, walked into the living room.

"Can I interrupt?" she asked.

I nodded. Ilene turned to Hans. "I guess I'd like to know what this is all about. Last night you showed slides of sheep and sang Yiddish songs. But what is the real relation?"

Hans leaned back in his chair and laughed. "Me. I am the relation."

Ilene crossed her arms. "But how does singing Yiddish songs go with shepherding in the Alps?" she asked.

"I like the songs," Hans said. "And I like very much to be shepherd. I like to stand in the mountains and to work with the dogs and the sheep."

"But why?" Ilene asked. "Why are you doing this show? Is it some kind of performance art?"

Hans squinted. "I do not know what is performance art."

"You know, performance art? Avant-garde? Conceptual stuff?"

"No, no. It is not this at all. I am not here because I am shepherd. I am here because I like to talk with people in Yiddish and to sing Yiddish songs."

Hans explained that when he first began to perform in the mid-1990s, he didn't mention the sheep or show slides. He sang mostly sad songs and spoke about his mother and the Nazis. These concerts took place in small cafés in Vienna, and Hans's friends and relatives made up a good portion of the crowd. But the cosmopolitan Viennese already knew what Yiddish was and had likely heard a few Yiddish songs. Hans wanted to bring Yiddish to the uninitiated in the Austrian Alps. Including the sheep in the show was simply a way to draw in the countryfolk who wouldn't otherwise be inclined to attend a Yiddish concert.

"The people in the countryside see me as their beloved shepherd because of all their associations with animals and their old roots," Hans said. "Only thirty or forty years ago, they all had to take care of some cows and so on. I wanted that they should come and listen and, perhaps for the first time in their lives, hear that there was Yiddish language."

I finally cut in. "So you want to make them remember?"

"No," Hans said, his eyes now fixed on mine. "I want to make them confront for the first time in their lives this culture that their uncles and fathers destroyed."

I went home that night and knocked out a thousand words on Hans for the English edition of the *Forward*, a famous Yiddish newspaper. But trying to convey Hans's story after one interview was harder than keeping a straight face during his concert. After my article appeared, I mailed it to Hans at his parents' apartment in Vienna with a note suggesting that I might like to visit him and write more about his life. Upon receiving my letter, Hans called me (the only time I spoke to him during the following year) and said that I was welcome to come whenever I liked.

I decided to travel to Austria because I was fascinated with Hans. I wanted to understand what had driven him to a life of wandering and to discover what it was like to be a shepherd in the twenty-first century. I wanted to make sense of Hans's Jewish identity, to appreciate what it really meant for him to sing in Yiddish.

But Hans wasn't the only object of my curiosity. Nine months before I met Hans, Austria's far-right Freedom Party, a direct descendant of the Austrian Nazi Party, had stunned Europe and the world by taking 27 percent of the national vote in the October 1999 parliamentary elections. An even bigger shock came four months later when the conservative People's Party announced it would form a governing coalition with the Freedom Party, meaning that an extremist party with Nazi roots would be at the seat of Austrian power. As soon as the new government formed, Israel pulled its ambassador out of Vienna and the European Union imposed diplomatic sanctions on Austria. *The New York Times* opined that "the Freedom Party's rhetoric, and the racist thinking behind it, has no place in the government of a European democracy."

There is good reason for the heightened sensitivity to far-right politics in Austria. Technically speaking, the Nazis invaded Austria on March 12, 1938, after Hitler ordered the German Eighth Army to cross Austria's northwestern border. But it was perhaps the most cordial invasion of one country by another in modern times. As German motorcades and infantry units passed through town after town, the citizens of Austria walked off their jobs to cheer the Nazi soldiers and shower them with flowers.

At the time Austria's Jewish community, almost all of it located in Vienna, accounted for approximately 185,000 of the country's 6 million citizens. The Viennese Jews were so well established and wealthy—they dominated a wide range of industries, from banking to the furniture trade, and comprised more than half of all doctors, lawyers, and dentists—that it seemed impossible to believe all their successes could be wiped out overnight.

But that is more or less what happened in the spring of 1938. With the Nazis firmly in power, the Viennese began attacking their Jewish neighbors with a murderous fervor. Even the German soldiers were shocked by what they saw—Germany's own anti-Jewish rioting seemed tame by comparison. Crowds cheered as gangs of storm troopers grabbed Jews from the sidewalks, beat them, and forced them to scrub the streets with toothbrushes. Synagogues were smashed and Jewish-owned stores ransacked. Jewish women were knocked down and pissed on. The white beards of rabbis were set afire for sport. On April 23, 1938, hundreds of Jews were marched to a famous Viennese amusement park where they were made to get down on their hands and knees and eat grass.

In the following years Austria would become a full-fledged part of the German Reich, and Hitler and Eichmann would turn out to be only the most famous Austrians with blood on their hands. Austrians accounted for 40 percent of the personnel in the Nazis' killing operations and provided more than one million soldiers for the German army.

The murders stopped with the end of World War II, but five and a half decades later 27 percent of Austrians had voted for a party founded by former Nazis, a party with a leader, Jörg Haider, who regularly vilified immigrants and who had a habit of making pro-Nazi statements. Was it possible that the Austrians' hatred of Jews had passed to the postwar generations, as though nothing had changed? Was Austria still, in some sense, a Nazi country? I wanted to find out.

⌐

My other reason for visiting Hans and his sheep was more personal. In writing about Yiddish culture and European anti-Semitism, I would be exploring the world of my grandmother Bashy, a world I inhabited for much of my childhood. Some of my earliest memories are of Bashy singing Yiddish lullabies to me as she pushed me along the sidewalks of suburban Houston in an old-fashioned buggy. There was "Patsh Zhe, Patsh Zhe, Kichelech":

*Patsh zhe, patsh zhe, kichelech*
*Der tate vet machn shichelech*
*Di mame vet shtrikn zekelech*
*Holts hakn, bulkes bakn, hiner tseyln*
*Morgn vet zayn a chasene.*

Clap, clap, cookies
Your father will make shoes
Your mother will knit socks
Chop wood, bake rolls, count the hens
Tomorrow there will be a wedding.

And then there was my favorite, "Unter Sams Viegeley" (any name could be substituted into the song):

*Unter Sams viegeley*
*Shteyt a vayser tsigele*
*Vos vet der tsigele handlen*
*Rozhinkes mit mandlen*
*Vos iz di beste schoyre*
*Di beste schoyre iz toyre mit rashe*
*Sam vet zogn a droshe*
*A sheyne droshe vet er zogn*
*Zayne matones vet er hobn*
*Shich un zokn vet er koyfn*
*Un in cheyder vet er loyfn.*

Under Sam's crib
Stands a white goat
What business is the goat in?
Raisins and almonds
What is the best merchandise?
The best merchandise is the Torah with Rashi [commentary]
Sam will give a good speech [at his bar mitzvah]
He'll give a good speech
He'll have presents
He'll buy shoes and socks
He'll run to Hebrew school.

I love these songs both because they remind me of Bashy and because I find the words a touching and funny reflection of what mattered most to my ancestors: Torah, weddings, small trades, and goats—probably in that order. It was a world

Bashy had left behind when she fled her Lithuanian shtetl at age eleven, but she had carried enough of it with her to give me a good taste.

Until I was old enough to drive, Bashy would pick me up from school every day, arriving an hour before classes ended and parking directly in front of the building. Since she wouldn't use the air conditioner in her tiny 1980 white Datsun (I spent countless hours trying to persuade her that doing so would not cause the car to go up in flames), she had to stand and wait outside. As soon as the bell rang, I would race to be the first one out, gesturing with my hand for Bashy to get back in the car so that no one would see my four-foot-ten-inch, white-haired grandmother trying to relieve me of my backpack.

After school we'd cruise around Houston together at twenty miles per hour, barely fast enough to generate a breeze through the car's open windows. Even other elderly drivers would zip past us, but Bashy never seemed to notice. Her eyes, hovering an inch above the steering wheel, stayed focused on the dangerous road ahead.

First we'd stop at the supermarket, where Bashy would sometimes introduce me to the confused cashiers as "my grandson, who keeps kosher." We'd buy the potatoes for Bashy's latkes and the flour and yeast for her challahs, then head to the bank, where Bashy liked to check in on the jewels in her safe-deposit box and where she would sometimes introduce me to the confused tellers as "my grandson, who keeps kosher."

Back at Bashy's home, a one-story obstacle course of antique furniture that always smelled of mothballs, I'd lie down on the couch and eat greasy potato latkes covered in cinnamon and sugar. Just as I was about to fall asleep, Bashy would yank up my head, shove a pillow underneath, and then wrap me in one of the *pooch perenis* (feather-filled comforters) she had managed to bring from the Old World. Once Bashy was convinced that she had attended to all my needs—food and warmth—she would sit down at the end of the couch, rub my feet, and tell me stories about her day: A policeman she encountered on her morning walk had told her that her jewelry was too beautiful and expensive to wear on the streets; the pump attendant at the gas station had told her that the strudel she had given him was better than anything his own mother made; the mailman couldn't believe how nice her roses were.

It was only as I grew older that I realized Bashy was embellishing these stories, that she and the policeman did not have a such a warm rapport and that the pump attendants at the gas station were not anxiously awaiting her next strudel delivery. What I didn't quite understand then, but see now, is that Bashy was reestablishing the order of the shtetl in suburban Houston. The folk characters had changed from the tailor and the shoemaker to the policeman and the pump attendant, but the mental landscape was largely the same.

And sprinkled throughout this landscape, like the raisins in the rock-hard challahs Bashy baked, was Yiddish. We spoke mostly in English, and so it was only as I got older that I realized that words like *chazeray* (junk) or *grepts* (burp) wouldn't be understood by anyone outside of my family. I've always liked the curses best: *gey kocken offen yom* (go shit in the ocean); *a geshvir dir in boych* (an ulcer in your entrails); *a krank dir in hartzn* (a sickness in your heart). But now I also appreciate the ritualistic use of the word *gezunt* (health).

Our family had a *gezunt* for every occasion. Before I left the house, it was *zay gezunt* (be healthy). If I were going on a trip, it was *for gezunt* (travel in health). At bedtime it was *shlof gezunt, shtey uf gezunt* (sleep in health, wake up in health). For a new piece of clothing it was *trog gezunt* (wear it in health). And so on.

And yet for all its tenderness, the landscape was not an entirely peaceful place, for the enemy—that is, the Gentiles—lived among us, and no matter how much she liked an individual *goy*, Bashy remained suspicious. Not even Mr. Newman, the elderly neighbor who helped her drag her garbage to the curb twice a week, was to be fully trusted. As far as Bashy was concerned, any non-Jew who strolled past her roses and up to her front door might just be dropping by to start a pogrom.

To prevent this pogrom, Bashy had six locks installed on her front door: two dead bolts, two chains, and two key locks. Visitors to the house were greeted by a floodlight that detected their arrival, then by Bashy's anxious eyes peering through the flowered curtains to the right of the front door. If Bashy recognized her guest and concluded that he was Jewish, or the rare welcomed *goy*, there was a long wait while she methodically unlocked the door, starting from the bolt at the top, which she could barely reach on her toes, and working her way down to the key in the doorknob.

Now and then I would time Bashy to see how long it would take her to undo all of the locks. But even as I teased her, the mentality that we were strangers among the *goyim* seeped in. Thanks to Bashy, I can't look at Christmas decorations without thinking *goyisheh naches* (something that gives the Gentiles pride or pleasure), and I feel guilty for even smelling the *treyf* (unkosher) aroma of a McDonald's bacon cheeseburger. It didn't happen often, but there were moments walking through the crowded halls of my public high school that I felt like a living anachronism, as though I belonged to a different time and place and had ended up in the late twentieth century among cowboy-boot-wearing Gentiles by mistake. I imagine a similar sense of disorientation is common to new immigrants, but I was born and raised in Houston. I'm a second-generation American on my father's side and a third-generation on my mother's side. I had every reason to be fully comfortable in my American skin, and yet deep down I knew that 99 percent of the people I saw on a daily basis were playing for the other team. Unlike Bashy, I could recognize the absurdity, recognize that the Gentiles in America were not out to get me. In fact, they were pretty nice. But I couldn't escape the dichotomy of Bashy's world. The distinction between Jew and goy was as sharp in my mind as it was in the mind of any self-respecting anti-Semite.

All of which is to say that when I left for Austria to think about Jews and Gentiles and anti-Semitism, I was carrying a lot more baggage than just my backpack. I didn't quite know what to expect when I left, but it wasn't long before I was up to my knees in sheep shit.

# Two

# A Neurotic Goes to Austria

On June 6, 2001, the day of my departure, I clicked my backpack closed and hopped in a cab to JFK International Airport. My plan was to walk with Hans and his sheep for a few weeks and then head to Vienna, where I would try to make sense of postwar anti-Semitism in Austria.

Everything appeared to be in place. I had a tape recorder and eighteen blank tapes. I had seven green-tinted steno notebooks. I had fifty pairs of disposable contact lenses. I had two hardcover library books on Austrian history and a travel book for tourists that included information on how to order *Schweinshaxe,* or "pork knuckles." I had twelve one-time-use toothbrush pads called Dental Dots that stick to the tip of the finger.

What I soon discovered I should have had but did not: a

regular toothbrush; hiking boots; wool socks; a heavy coat; a rain jacket; rain pants; a sweater; deodorant; a watch; press credentials; a small satchel so that I would not have had to show up to interview a prominent Viennese politician with my notebooks and tapes in a garbage bag.

The flight to Austria was uneventful. That said, one should be aware that if you ever order a vegetarian meal on Austrian Airlines, you will likely get two servings of fruit for breakfast. One serving will be in a cup, the other in a bowl. But they will be identical servings down to the number of grapes.

When I disembarked and retrieved my backpack from the luggage carousel, I found that the top was covered in a strange semenlike substance. While I'm fairly certain it was not semen, the thought that one of the airport baggage people had ejaculated on my backpack put a bad taste in my mouth as I nervously looked for Hans. I noticed that I had an old tag from El Al, Israel's national airline, on my bag, and it occurred to me that this possible masturbatory attack on my backpack may, in fact, have been an anti-Semitic masturbatory attack.

After several minutes of scanning the faces around me, I spotted a brown wool hat with a brim that circled the head and extended outward at least a foot (think floppy sombrero). As this is not the type of hat you expect to see a non-shepherd wearing in an airport, I wasn't surprised to find a smiling Hans beneath the enormous brim. We hugged briefly. We didn't know each other well enough to hug, but a hug somehow felt mandatory after an international flight.

Hans's hair was much shorter in the back, but his sideburns remained substantial. He wore navy blue pants with a splattering of mud on the right leg and a faded black T-shirt. Although I had not noticed the similarities before, the small wrinkles beneath his eyes and the rounded tip of his nose now reminded me of my father.

Hans and I exchanged pleasantries as we walked to his blue minivan, inside of which were two giant bags of salt, five or six shepherd's sticks that looked as though they had been carved from branches, old boots and work clothes, the squealing puppies of one of the sheepdogs, and an assortment of Yiddish folk tapes. The van had a faint odor of excrement, and I wondered whether it was the puppies or just the natural smell of a shepherd's van.

"You want to drink?" Hans asked, opening a carton of orange juice and sniffing it.

"No thanks," I said.

I tried to make myself comfortable in the passenger's seat, opening the window a crack to counteract the smell.

"When you are in Vienna, you will stay with my parents or my girlfriend," Hans said as we pulled out of the parking lot. His hat was now off, and his brown hair was matted to his head.

"I already have reservations at a hostel," I said, wondering who this girlfriend might be. As far as I knew, Hans was happily married.

"This is not necessary," Hans responded. "You will be my guest when you are in Austria, and when I am coming with my girlfriend to New York, we will stay with you."

I pictured 625 sheep crammed into my tiny Upper West Side walk-up.

"Um, okay," I said. Hans's self-invitation had startled me, but I was secretly relieved. A few days before I left, I had searched the Internet for photos of my hostel's rooms. I found the hostel's webpage, but instead of the rooms, a large picture of two bare-chested men, one embracing the other from behind, popped up on the screen. I had inadvertently made reservations at Vienna's only gay hostel.

As we drove from Vienna's airport that morning, heading toward the flock, I got my first glimpse of the Austrian countryside. About 100 kilometers south of Vienna, the crop fields of Lower Austria begin to give way to Alpine foothills, a horizon of green waves that made even a cynic like me feel euphoric. I wouldn't have minded stopping for a few minutes to take in the view, but there was no time. We were an hour behind schedule, and Hans's wife, Kati (pronounced Kä-ti), was waiting for us with two of their three children, Andreas, fourteen, and Wolfi, nine. (Hans's eldest son, Günter, sixteen, was living with his grandparents in Vienna while working as an apprentice to a carpenter.)

Strapped into the passenger's seat, my small black backpack wedged between my legs, I tried to think of something to say. I'm shy and bad at small talk, but I found it especially hard to chat with Hans because we seemingly had so little in common. I'm American. He's Austrian. My knowledge of music is limited mostly to old-school hip-hop. Hans is an expert in the real old school: Yiddish folk. I don't wear my glasses despite my poor vision because I'm convinced it's impossible to balance the lenses evenly on the bumpy bridge of my nose. Hans walks around airports in a gigantic shepherd's hat.

"Do your sons enjoy working as shepherds?" I asked.

"Yes, they like it very much," Hans said, his eyes on the road. He didn't seem unhappy, but his face is rarely without shades of pain. "My son Andi is very good shepherd," Hans said. "Perhaps he will take over the flock one day."

I had forgotten just how rough Hans's English could be. He has a large vocabulary and is rarely difficult to comprehend, but he never mastered the finer points of the language. "The's," "this's," and "that's" are interchangeable in his speech. Short "i's" usually end up as long "e's" so that "ill" becomes "eel" and "bird" becomes "beerd." Prepositions come and go without warning.

Before I had the chance to ask another question, Hans's cell phone rang, and he strapped on a headset. During the two-hour drive from the airport to the sheep, Hans received at least a half dozen calls. I thought of the old AT&T cell phone commercials in which a shepherd walks through the countryside with a phone in one hand and his stick in the other. Presumably, AT&T wanted us to find humor in this juxtaposition of ancient and modern, but I can now say with authority that there is nothing funny about a wandering shepherd's reliance upon the cell phone, or "handy," as they call it in Austria. Hans says that his handy has changed his life by allowing him to stay in touch with friends and search for places to stay as he moves with the sheep.

While Hans chatted and repeatedly said "*ja, ja*" into the mouthpiece of his handy's headset, I worried about how to tell him that I was a vegetarian. It was only a matter of time before the subject came up, and I thought my refusal to eat meat might offend him—after all, he makes his living by selling lambs for food.

"Please don't feel you have to make any special arrangements for me," I said when Hans put down his phone, "but just so you know, I don't eat meat."

Hans smiled. "You are vegetarian," he said. "I suspected this."

What did that mean? Was my fear that Hans thought of me as a wimpy American city slicker proving true?

"This is not problem," Hans continued. "You will eat cheese and eggs, yes?"

"Yes," I said. I don't particularly like cheese, but I had decided in advance that it would be better to eat things I don't like than to carry fifteen boxes of soy burgers with me, as I had done for years at the all-boys sports camp I attended as an adolescent. In those days I still ate meat, but the camp was not Jewish and didn't offer any kosher selections. On the first day, while the other boys dragged their duffel bags to the bunks, I would hurry to the kitchen with my bright red cooler to make sure my veggie patties made it to the freezer before thawing.

We drove in silence for some time, then Hans began to sing a mournful Yiddish ditty under his breath. I asked him what the song meant. "It is a song about a tailor who is waiting for the holidays so he can put away his needle and go to synagogue," Hans said.

Even without the slides of the sheep in the background, I couldn't help but find it funny that Hans, who I knew had had a Communist upbringing and who I suspected had never uttered a prayer in his life, was singing centuries-old songs about a longing for synagogue. But amused or not, I liked listening to Hans sing. And I loved the way a simple mention of Yiddish could fill his voice with tenderness. Although I hadn't fully grasped this at the time, Hans's attachment to Yiddish borders on obsession. When I left Austria, I flew to Israel, and before going to the airport I asked Hans if he would like anything from the Jewish state. I was thinking of a menorah or perhaps a framed photograph of the Western Wall. Hans asked if I might walk around with my tape recorder and ask the old people I encountered in the streets if they knew any old Yiddish songs.

After singing for a bit, Hans announced he had a story he wanted to share. Several days before I met him for the first time in New York, Hans had been in Canada for the annual KlezKanada klezmer festival. During a break from the festival, Hans spent an afternoon touring a Jewish neighborhood in Montreal. As he strolled the residential streets, three separate elderly women stopped to talk to him. The conversations were insignificant. But something about these old women, Hans said, was *"heymish."* *Heymish* is the Yiddish word for "deeply familiar" or "homey." Hans had never had a feeling quite like it. And what struck Hans most of all about these women were their hands. Unlike the coarse, thick hands of the Austrians, they were delicate and bony, the hands of intellectuals. They were, in Hans's eyes, typically Jewish, *heymish* hands that reminded him of the hands of his father.

After telling me this story, Hans was quick to add that if he were to use the expression "typical Jewish hands" in Austria, he would be attacked by his leftist friends. In fact, when he had tried to explain the hands to a Jewish friend, she had told him he was being ridiculous. I tended to agree, but I was intrigued by Hans's anxiousness to manufacture a Jewish connection to the old women. The more he spoke about Yiddish or Judaism, the more of a mystery he seemed.

"Did your father teach you anything at all about Judaism?" I asked. In the distance, snowcapped peaks cut through an increasingly cloudy sky.

"My father was not interested in Judaism," Hans said, then made a face that was something between a wince and a smirk. "When I was a child, I could not even pronounce the word 'Jew.' In German it is *Jud* or *Jude*. It took me twenty years to learn to speak out this word, and still I cannot do it without contradictory emotions."

I reached behind me and moved a shepherd's stick that was pushing into the back of my seat.

"You mean your father wouldn't allow you to even talk about Jews?"

"No, it is not like this. You must understand how this word was used in this country," Hans said. "I grew up before '68, and it was establishment everywhere. In that world, if you would say the word *Jud*, it would be like you say 'whore' or 'son of whore' or 'motherfucker' or something like this. This word was the word the Nazis put on Jewish stores and on their drawings of Jews. It was so loaded and there was such bad national consciousness surrounding it that even to pronounce this word was not possible. Only fascists or uninformed people who really think that Jews are the evil of the world could use it in this old sense. The first time I remember hearing it, I was in elementary school. The children teased small girl with almond eyes. I made defense of her, and they turned to me and shouted, *'Jud. Jud.'* I went home and asked my parents what this word means."

Hans had said "son of whore" and "motherfucker," but the better parallel in the United States, I thought, was "nigger." Calling someone a Jew in postwar Austria was like calling someone a nigger in the United States.

"So what word did you use to talk about Jews?"

Hans turned to me with a halfhearted smile. "In this country you did not talk about Jews for many years."

Didn't talk about Jews? For my family that would have been like not breathing. But as strange as this sounded to me, the next thing Hans said surprised me even more. "You must understand that I was also German speaking and part of the German-speaking people. I was child of victims, of a leftist and a Jew, but I also felt part of it. I had a bad consciousness for years just because I was speaking German. When I went to Poland for the first time, all I could think of was how many people had been killed there and how many Polish children had been robbed by the Germans."

Hans's handy rang, cutting off the lesson like the bell in a classroom. It was Kati, wondering where we were. As Hans spoke into his headset, I tried to process what he had just told me. How could Hans of all people feel responsible for German crimes? Was it possible that his turn to Yiddish was not so much a search for his roots as a search for atonement?

When Hans took off his headset, I wanted to resume our conversation, but after talking to Kati, Hans looked as though someone had just punched him in the stomach. The whole structure of his face sunk, and he let out a defeatist puff of air.

"When we get to the sheep, you will meet Kati. You must understand there is great tension between us."

"What kind of tension?" I asked.

Hans looked at me. "I am hot, and she is cold. You know what I mean by this?"

"Not really," I admitted.

"When I was younger," Hans said, "you could put warm bowl of soup on my lap and I would get erection."

"Uh-huh," I mumbled, somewhat nervously. I had no idea how we had gotten here. Hans's life seemed strange enough to me without this new tidbit.

"With Kati, I would want to have sex every day, but she is not like this," Hans said. "Sometimes she did not want sex."

I nodded and squeezed my backpack between my knees. Why was this man telling me about his sex life?

"For a long time I had very bad complex," Hans continued. "I thought there was something wrong with me. Now I understand that it is not wrong to want sex very often. People are different. Some want more than others."

"So does Kati know about your girlfriend?"

"Yes, yes," Hans said. "She knows. She also has boyfriend. A dentist in Styria. It is very complicated because we spend so much time together with the sheep and are sleeping sometimes very near each other so that over the winter we grew a little bit close again. But now this dentist tells her she cannot go near me anymore." You could hear the spite in Hans's voice when he said the word "dentist."

"So why do the two of you work with the sheep together?"

"Because this is our way of life," Hans said, sounding slightly defensive. "We both are shepherds, and we both like very much to work with the sheep."

"Oh," I said.

If any other man had told me his powerful libido had ruined his relationship, I would have written it off as machismo. But Hans hardly seemed worried about appearing manly. When I first interviewed him in Brooklyn, Hans told me that Yiddish appealed to him because it was "the language of the heart." Besides, machismo is the mask of masculinity. Hans, it was becoming increasingly clear, wore no masks at all. Call it artifice, call it civility, but whatever it is, Hans didn't seem to have it. I had never met anyone like him. He was painfully honest and, in his honesty, painfully vulnerable.

As we drove on, cars that all looked a little too small occasionally joined us on the open road. Hans asked me if I had boots for the mountains. "I think these will do," I said, lifting my foot and showing him my designer Australian boots. I had bought the boots to impress a girl I was dating, and somewhat to my amazement, it had worked. She had thought I was cool (at least until she discovered that I had stopped resting my laptop computer on my lap for fear that it was irradiating my genitals). But there was no fooling Hans.

"We will find you real boots to wear," Hans said. I looked at Hans's feet. He was again wearing sandals over socks. *Not so hot either,* I thought. I also noticed for the first time that Hans's T-shirt said SHAQ on the front in white letters. Finally, a perfect vehicle for lighthearted chitchat.

"So you're a basketball fan?" I asked.

Hans looked at me.

"Shaquille O'Neal," I said. "The Shaq?"

Hans looked at me again.

"Your shirt."

Hans glanced down with a confused expression, then told me that he rarely buys clothes and that he didn't even know where this shirt had come from.

I explained that Shaquille O'Neal is the most dominant basketball player in the world, that when he is near the basket, no one can stop him. Hans seemed interested. Later I would point out the mostly faded silk screen of Shaq's face on the back of his shirt. "It is funny," Hans said. "All this time I did not know there was black man on my shirt."

Half an hour later Hans and I pulled up to a two-story white farmhouse with brown wood shutters. In front of the house was a pile of wood big enough to keep a fireplace going for about a decade. I was expecting to see the sheep grazing nearby, but it turned out to be only a pit stop. "This is the house of my friends," Hans said. "We will eat here quickly, and I will find you boots." We walked into a large kitchen with dark oak floors and wood-paneled walls. Hans introduced me to Manfred and Lore. Manfred was tall and ruggedly handsome, with a strong jaw and thick gray hair. With the addition of a cowboy hat, he might have passed for an Austrian Marlboro Man. Lore had reddish brown hair pulled back in a ponytail and small features that were shriveling with age. Neither of them spoke English, but Lore, like a number of elderly Austrian women I would meet, managed to communicate by saying the words *ja* and *bitte* constantly while gesturing with her hands. (*Bitte* is the German word for "please." It can also be used for "you're welcome.")

Lore "*bitted*" me over to the table, and Manfred, who had just finished chopping wood, disappeared in search of boots and clothes for me. Hans told Lore that I would have only cheese on my sandwich. She looked concerned, let out a few *bittes*, and retreated to the kitchen.

After lunch, during which Hans downed two large turkey sandwiches on thick slabs of brown country bread, it was time to dress me. "You must have good clothes," Hans said. "It might rain today, and tomorrow we will go over the big mountain."

"Big mountain?" I asked.

"Yes," Hans said. "It is very big mountain. You will like it."

I wasn't so sure. I had last done serious hiking in the north of Israel with a friend. After a wonderful afternoon of traversing jagged rocks and leaping over streams, I had dropped to my hands and knees and vomited three times. I ended up hitchhiking to a hospital, and as we drove, I told the driver in my broken Hebrew to hurry because I had lost all feeling in my hands. I was given an IV for dehydration at the hospital and I quickly recovered, but ever since I've wondered if summer hikes are perhaps a bad idea for me. In addition to my proclivity for dehydration, I'm prone to heatstrokes. And although inhalers seem to have little effect, it's believed (granted, only by me) that I have exercise-induced asthma.

Manfred returned to the kitchen smiling and holding up a pair of dark blue ski overalls. They looked small, but I climbed into them, lifting the straps up and over my shoulders. Unaccustomed to wearing overalls, I couldn't seem to make the outfit work, and the next thing I knew, Hans and Manfred were both pulling at various pieces of my clothing and laughing. I began to sense that the thought of me working as a shepherd was as absurd to them as it was to me.

Next it was time to step into Manfred's boots. They were large brown work boots, which turned out to be as big on me as the overalls were small. Fortunately, Manfred also had several extra pairs of wool socks. Hans then produced a child-sized striped baseball cap and plopped it on my head. I looked like an overgrown toddler playing in a grown-up's shoes.

Hans also had to change before we left, and I waited for him outside, where several dogs were running around. One, a mutt with a short black coat, was especially frisky. He brought me a stick in his mouth, and soon we were engaged in a heated round of tug-of-war. The dog put up a good fight, but he was no match for me. I yanked the stick away and threw it into the distance. The dog ran after it and brought it back. *All right*, I thought, *one more*. I reached down for the stick, pulled it away, and then, just to add a little drama, I waved the stick in front of the dog's face, at which point he bit my hand.

The wound was small, causing only a drop or two of blood, and my breathing remained normal for a moment. Then I realized I might have rabies. I hurried inside to announce that I had been injured.

"The dog," I said, pointing to my hand.

Manfred shook his head. He understood a little English. "This is stupid dog," he said.

"Yes," I said. "But maybe he has a disease?"

"This is stupid dog," Manfred said again. "He likes to play too much."

*Yes, yes*, I thought. *Stupid, sure. All dogs are stupid.* But did this stupid dog happen to have a disease that was going to cause me to start foaming at the mouth?

"Rabies?" I said. "This dog maybe has rabies?"

The message wasn't getting through. "Lore will help you," Hans interjected, and the next thing I knew, I was biting my lips as a stern-faced Lore dabbed my wound with iodine and wrapped it in gauze.

I gave up trying to communicate my fears and walked back outside. Hans emerged in a surprisingly sporty rain suit, and we were off. But nothing was the same from then on. There was a big mountain to look forward to, and dehydration and rabies, and this was all in addition to the slipped disk in my back, which was pressing on my sciatic nerve and occasionally causing a horrible shooting pain down my right leg.

When we were just minutes from the flock, Hans told me that he had "only been half shepherd" thus far because he had been away from the sheep. Now he was "going to be full shepherd," which meant that he might be too busy "speaking with the dogs" or moving the sheep out of the way of traffic to talk to me. I was given the choice of walking ahead of the flock—always making sure I never broke the cardinal rule of passing between the shepherd and his sheep—or walking behind the sheep as a lamb herder. I chose to be a lamb herder.

# Three

# Vienna Dreams

Bashy and I are in Vienna. We are summer tourists, and we are staying in Vienna's only gay hostel. I made the reservations by mistake, but now that we are here, we are comfortable.

Frank, the man at the reservations desk, is all muscle. He wears tight V-necked T-shirts and speaks in a thick German accent. When I ask him if he goes to the gym a lot, he says, "Ja, ja."

Bashy and I are tourists in only the broadest sense. We do no touring.

Sometimes I plead with Bashy to go downtown with me.

"What's there to see?" Bashy says.

"The museums," I say. "The famous buildings, the people."

"Goyishce nachas," *Bashy says.*

*In the lobby of the hostel is a restaurant where they sell* Sachertortes *and warm* Apfelstrudel. *I am not to eat at this restaurant. Bashy has brought cans of oily tuna and her own strudel wrapped in aluminum foil. We eat on paper plates at a small wooden table in our room. When the maids come to clean, Bashy shoos them out.* "Prostitutes," *she calls them in Yiddish.*

*Frank is the only Austrian Bashy likes. When he brings us clean towels, Bashy forces him to take a piece of strudel.* "He's a mensch," *Bashy says.*

"Your grandmother is so teeny," *Frank says.*

*One afternoon, while I am finishing my strudel, I make a stand.* "Bashy," *I say,* "I'm twenty-five years old. There's a world out there."

"Finish your strudel," *Bashy says.*

*I finish my strudel, but I am still hungry. I tell Bashy that I'm going to go out and explore downtown Vienna.*

*Bashy sees it in my eyes that I am serious.* "Let Frank go with you," *she says.*

"I don't want to go with Frank," *I say.*

"Fine, so I'll go," *Bashy says.*

*I go downtown with Frank. I look at the spires of the cathedrals and the legs of the women. I almost buy a torte. Frank takes me to an upscale bar. He buys me drinks and squeezes my biceps.*

"Frank, I'm not gay," *I say.*

"Ja, I never said your were," *Frank says.*

*I apologize, but Frank is not having it. He stands up and leaves the bar.*

*I walk through downtown alone, and when I make it*

*back to the hostel, Frank and Bashy are waiting in the lobby. Bashy doesn't have her false teeth in. Her lips are folded into her face.*

*"Where were you?" Bashy asks.*

*"Just walking," I say.*

*"You could have been killed," Bashy says.*

*"It's not dangerous," I say. "Tell her, Frank."*

*Frank looks at me in disgust. "You have muscles like girl," he says.*

Four

# Meet the Sheep

The sheep were still two weeks shy of their summer pasture
in southwestern Styria. Styria, one of Austria's nine *Laen-
der*, or provinces, begins in the southeast tip of Austria and
cuts a large swath through the center of the country. According to Styria's official website, "Green colors the self-image
of the province, in which cheerful optimism is more often the
case than resignation." Although Hans's route changes
every year depending on the weather and where he can find
the best grass, since 1992 he has been making the same
broad loop with the sheep, spending summers in Styria and
winters in Lower Austria.

Hans and I were meeting the flock just north of Knittelfeld, a small town set amid the soft green slopes of Styria's
Mur valley. Our long drive was almost over. Hans turned off

the freeway and followed a winding road for about ten minutes until we came to the foot of a long meadow, lined by a small paved path on one side and woods on the other. The stretch of grass directly in front of me was vacant, but when I looked up, there they were, spread out over 100 yards like 625 woolly players nibbling on a football field.

The expanse of sheep left me breathless for a moment. Their coats were every shade from dark brown to off-white. Their legs were mostly still, but their mouths were in constant motion, a flurry of gums and grass. Some had well-kept short wool. Others looked like they were in desperate need of a good shearing, their thick "sheep-fro's" sprouting in every direction.

But what really struck me were the faces, long and pointy and much more horselike than I had remembered from childhood visits to petting zoos. At the tip of a sheep's head is a shiny black nose with nostrils that arc upward like butterfly wings and a mouth that, when closed, looks like it might have a tennis ball lodged inside. But the eyes are arguably the strangest part of the sheep countenance. They are set so far to the sides of the head that you can never really look a sheep straight on. It gives the sheep an almost sinister air. In contrast to the lamb as a metaphor for peacefulness, these eyes made me think that I would not want to run into a sheep in a dark alley late at night.

And then there are their lovely ears, which flap freely up and down whenever the sheep move. At rest, the ears neither stick up nor hang down, but point outward at almost ninety-degree angles from the head, so that if you were to draw a line from the mouth to the tips of the ears, you'd have an isosceles triangle. Some of the ears were encircled by wool at the base (I found these more distinguished); others were shorn to give the ears a bit more breathing room.

Still, intrigued as I was by the sheep, I can't say I found them sexually exciting. Before I left for Austria, a surprising number of my friends had made jokes about me copulating with a ewe. I laughed along but kept wondering why people have the idea that men like having sex with sheep. What is it about sheep, as opposed to the much more available dogs or cats? Why not turkeys for that matter? Or moose? Or baboons? I asked Hans about this sheep sex phenomenon several days later, and he said he had never heard of it until he traveled to North America.

As I took in the sheep from the side of the road, Hans ran ahead to talk to Kati, who was standing at the front of the flock in the distance. I was alone, and the moment I'd been anticipating had finally arrived: I opened the van's sliding side door and grabbed a shepherd's stick. Despite all my anxieties (I was still checking my dog bite every few minutes for signs of rabies), I've never been able to entirely rid my imagination of scenes of personal triumph. In the shepherd fantasy I entertained before my trip, I'm standing in front of the flock, my stick raised high in the air. I don't have to say a word. The sheep know to follow. Hans is nowhere to be found. It's just me and the sheep, and when the sun goes down, I walk into a conveniently placed cave and build a fire. Then, as luck would have it, I encounter a beautiful mountain woman. She asks if she can stay the night in my cave. I tell her she's making a terrible mistake. "I am a wandering shepherd," I say. "No matter what happens tonight, I will wake up in the morning and move on." "I don't care," she says. "I want to make love to you all night." "Great," I say, then I ask her if she's been tested for HIV and if she, perhaps, has some paperwork to prove it.

Hans and Kati walked over to me, and Hans made the introductions. Kati's skinny arms dangled out of her tank top. She had blue eyes, a dark tan, and straight brown hair down to her shoulders. Despite her sun-worn skin, her beauty was unmistakable. After saying hello, Kati walked to the front of the flock, and Hans and I were alone for a moment. He sat down on the bumper of the van and looked up at me. "Kati just now tells me that if I should try to touch her one more time, she is leaving the flock forever," Hans said. He had that same punched-in-the-stomach look I had seen in the van.

I didn't know what to say. I felt sorry for Hans. I know the sting of rejection as well as the next guy, the pit in the stomach, the dry mouth, the absolute belief that happiness is an illusion. In fact, I had one additional reason for traveling to Austria. I was escaping the fallout of my own romantic disasters.

Until my early twenties, women took little interest in me. It may just have been that they weren't attracted to me, but it may also have had something to do with my approach to courting. Only in college did it really sink in that to meet a woman I would first have to speak to a woman. I was so quiet in high school that a group of girls began to refer to me behind my back as "Sad Sam." I wanted to tell them that I wasn't especially sad, just shy, but I was too shy even to explain the distinction. What those girls couldn't know was that I wanted nothing more than to befriend them. I would sometimes fantasize about sitting at their lunch table and making funny asides. *Sam, I had no idea you could be so lively,* Amy would say, a strip of Fruit Roll-Up disappearing behind her full red lips. *I love you,* I would respond.

My loneliness won out over my shyness in the end, and I found myself in a solid relationship during my senior year of college. But when my girlfriend and I moved to different cities after graduation, I began to date periodically, and I wasn't very good at it. Things might start well, but eventually it would become clear that I was not joking, that I really wasn't going to eat the lettuce at the salad bar because it was right next to the little cubes of ham ("For God's sake, there's no ham in the lettuce, Sam!"), and that I really was afraid to sleep under framed posters (apparently, I'm the only person in the world who finds the prospect of being awakened one night by a plate of glass shattering on one's face unappealing).

Then, in the year before my trip, something strange and wholly unexpected began to happen. Either because of a shortage of eligible men in New York City or because I had discovered that a touch of gel could bring a semblance of order to the anarchy on my head, a number of women seemed interested in having a relationship with me. This should have been spectacular news, should have been reason to sprint up and down Broadway pumping my fists in the air while humming the theme music to *Rocky*. But there was a problem: I was more than happy to be the boyfriend of these women, but because they didn't like my favorite books, or because they liked my least favorite books, or because they believed in vaguely defined spiritual forces, or because they used words like "insidious" without irony, or because they said "you're so funny" in a way that revealed they didn't think I was so funny, I didn't particularly want to marry any of them. At the time this struck me as a serious moral dilemma, and I concluded that the only defensible option was to mention, on the very first date, that I didn't want to get married.

The woman's response would always be, "Don't worry about it, I don't want to marry you either," to which I'd say, "Fine, then there's no problem." And things would progress. We'd go out to dinner and pretend to talk like pirates. We'd read short stories aloud to each other until our voices grew hoarse. We'd have sex. A month or so later I would offer a casual reminder that I didn't think the relationship had "long-term potential," at which point I would be called a bastard and asked to leave the apartment.

It was after a particularly nasty breakup that the answer to my dilemma came to me: traveling. Only when you're traveling can you date someone you don't intend to spend the rest of your life with and not feel guilty. The escape is built into the arrangement. Ending things doesn't mean you're a bad person. You just have to go home. I was so taken with this insight that I never stopped to think that I myself might be the one to get attached. Even stranger, I never stopped to think that there might be a contradiction between my search for anti-Semites and my search for an Austrian woman.

———

"You will go with the boys," Hans said. "They will show you what to do."

Hans walked some fifty yards ahead to the front of the
flock, where Kati was already stationed, and started belting
out "Hey, Tsigelech," the song he opened with at his concert
in New York. Once you understand Hans's relationship to
Kati, the lyrics take on new meaning:

> Hey, little goats, come here quickly
> I will now sing you a pretty song:
> It begins with a shepherd and a girl that bewitched him.
> Hey, little goats, hear what happened:
> The shepherd was once cheerful and lively,
> Now he is sad, does not glance at the sheep,
> but yearns for the girl who bewitched him.
> Hey, little goats, listen to the end of the song:
> Like orphans his poor flock wanders about.
> The little shepherd lies deep in the lake
> and the girl sits by the water and cries.

*"Tsigelech"* is an appropriate call to the animals because
there are two goats in the flock—included for their leadership
skills. Unlike the sheep, the goats always keep one eye on
Hans, and when it's time to continue forward, they don't try
to sneak in a few more nibbles. They move ahead and the
sheep follow. I came to have great respect for these two goats,
one bearded, the other horned. If Hans and Kati were king
and queen of the flock, the goats were their ministers and the
sheep the loyal subjects. The boys were the princes, I suppose, and the sheepdogs their knights. I'm not sure what that
made me—perhaps the jester or the court Jew?

As Hans and Kati walked ahead, I made my way over to
Andi and Wolfi, who were standing behind the sheep. Andi
was shy and Wolfi didn't speak English, so there was no conversation, let alone instruction.

Wolfi, classically cute with short brown bangs and a toothy smile, held a shepherd's stick about a foot taller than he was. (All the shepherd's sticks tended to be a foot taller than their carriers, and Wolfi's had been shortened accordingly.) Andi had straight brown hair down to his shoulders and gentle brown eyes. He was hardly intimidating, but his angry *hop hops* made me jump.

Most of the sheep seemed to understand that a *hop hop* from Andi meant, *Enough chewing, let's move on out.* But every now and then one animal would ignore the call, and then Andi repeated the *hops* in an even angrier tone. If an unusually bold sheep still wouldn't budge, Andi would take his stick and throw it at the sheep like a javelin. He didn't usually hit them, but I was taken aback. Wolfi, meanwhile, was running around stabbing his stick into the ground and leaping forward as though practicing for a miniature pole vault competition. It began to feel like I was in the lamb-herding Olympics.

We passed from the field into the dense forest ahead, and I discovered that lamb herding can be an extremely difficult job. The sheep inevitably disappeared behind bushes and trees, and just when it seemed as though they were all accounted for, one last lamb would come racing from behind to catch up with the others. I was glad that I had brought my newly purchased disposable contacts, even if it did take twenty minutes to put them in every morning. Good vision is important for the lamb herder not only because he or she must scan for wayward sheep or because the lamb herder, unlike the shepherd, walks in the path of fresh shit, but also because the lamb herder must be able to see the signals from the shepherd far ahead. When Hans wanted us to move slowly, he lifted then lowered his hand; to speed us up, he moved his outstretched arm from side to side. If he wanted us to be extra careful not to leave a lamb behind, he placed his hand above his eyes, as though blocking out the sun.

I followed Hans's orders, but I hated bothering the flock while they were eating. I kept wondering what it would be like if I had to eat all of my meals with a shouting giant hovering over me with a stick. I felt especially bad hurrying the little lambs. Some of them were only a few weeks old and still had a little wobble in their stride. I knew I had to do my fair share of *hop hop*ing if I was going to garner any respect from the boys or the sheep, but it's not the type of work I'm cut out for. I'm soft-spoken, with a deep crackly voice, so much so that people always assume they're waking me when I answer the phone. In addition, I'm physically incapable of screaming. At some point in junior high, word of my handicap got out, and my classmates found it fascinating. On the playground, groups of preteens would come up to me and ask me to make the loudest noise I could. All I ever managed was a sort of George of the Jungle *"Ahhaahhh,"* which would, of course, send everyone into fits of giggles.

With practice, I got my *hop hop*s to a near shout, but the sheep never really responded to me the way they did to Andi. Usually they would give me these "You call that a *hop hop*?" looks and continue eating, leaving me feeling like the substitute teacher whose very presence signals the absence of authority. Later I became fixated on the question of whether there was anything integral to the noise *hop hop* that the sheep were responding to or if *hap hap* or *heep heep* would

work just as well. When no one was around, I would test these new noises out, but I never did come to a satisfactory answer because the sheep tended to ignore me either way.

By contrast, I paid great attention to the sheep's bleating. They *baaah*ed much more loudly and nasally than you'd expect. A few of the stronger bleaters, I thought, might have had second careers as foghorns. The *baaah*s—or *beeeh*s, more precisely—would be intermittent until feeding time. Then, suddenly, dozens of ewes would cry out at once to their lambs in an ear-ringing chorus of animal need.

While I was busy listening to the *baaah*ing and bossing around two-week-old lambs, Churka was doing the real work. Churka was one of Hans's and Kati's three *Altdeutsche Schäferhunde* (Old German shepherd dogs). The *Altdeutscher Schäferhund*, so named because it has been the dog of choice of shepherds in Germany since medieval times, is the ancestor of the modern German shepherd dog. Now nearly extinct, the *Altdeutscher Schäferhund* was bred to a standard only in 1989 and can look like a wide array of different breeds, from poodles to schnauzers. Churka, medium-sized, with a shaggy gray and white coat, resembled a border collie.

As the sheep shuffled along, Churka would race back and forth along one side of the flock, tracing an imaginary border that the sheep were not to cross. If a sheep managed to stray so far that it didn't make it back inside the border before Churka arrived on the scene, Churka and the sheep would face off like a linebacker and a running back. The sheep, sometimes faking one way and going the other, would try to scurry back into the flock without Churka clutching a leg in her teeth. When I first witnessed one of these standoffs, I was startled by Churka's ferocity and felt sorry for the sheep. But Hans explained that the dogs only "grip" the sheep in places where the wool is thick and that his animals are never injured. Hans trains his puppies to grip by draping a lamb in a raincoat with holes cut out to expose the appropriate targets. (Note: If you ever happen to be hiking the Alps and you see a man singing Yiddish songs as he watches a dog chasing a sheep in a raincoat, no need for concern.)

Every few minutes Churka would stop and look up at Hans, who would point his stick and bark out rapid-fire commands in an intensely nasal voice, always saying the dog's name before the command: "Churka, *steh* [stand]!"

"Churka, *draussen* [outside]!" "Churka, *bleib* [stay]!" "Churka, *ab* [go]!" You could never tell when these commands were coming, so a typical conversation with Hans while he's with the sheep is a bit like talking to someone with Tourette's: "I'm remember when I was—Churka, *bleib!* Churka, *ab! Churka, komm 'rum (herum), und hopp! ab ins Feld!*—little and I was talking with . . ."

Sounding a bit like Tolstoy, Hans once declared that "the only dogs that are happy are shepherd dogs. All other dogs are unhappy." He based this statement on his belief that canine contentedness is dependent upon bending to wolfish instincts. To ensure that his dogs are in touch with their inner wolves, Hans always lets them go a little hungry when they work. As Hans put it, if you feed the sheepdog before work in the morning, "the dog will be seelly all the day and not understand you." Still, the sheepdogs can't go too hungry, or else they really will kill the sheep.

⌒

We emerged from the thicket of trees and shrubs onto a mountain road with a small stream a few yards off to the right. It was only about 3:00 P.M., but the sky had turned gray, and it looked as though it would rain at any minute. I was beginning to develop a bit of a shepherding rhythm. The mountains draped in softly drooping evergreens and the urinelike trickle of the stream, where the bolder sheep would scamper off to drink, distracted me from the vision of an angry Austrian nurse administering multiple rabies shots to my stomach. We ascended the winding road slowly until we reached a spot near a farmhouse with enough space for the sheep to spread out and graze. By the time I arrived from the back, Hans was sitting on a log, eating an apple. I joined him.

"Do you want an apple, Sam Apple?" Hans asked, holding out an apple and laughing. "I think it is not the first time you get this question. But take, it is a good apple from farmer."

I took the apple and sat down. We had been walking for only a few hours, but my feet were already sore from Manfred's boots. Kati and Wolfi drove ahead in Kati's white Jeep to set up the sheep's fence for the evening, and Andi found a quiet spot of his own. Hans and I sat in silence for a moment eating our apples and watching the sheep. Then Hans caught me staring at his stick. "You want I should tell you about the stick?" he asked.

"Yes," I said. It's hard to make it through seven years of Hebrew school without a little curiosity about a shepherd's stick. Shepherd imagery permeates the Old Testament: Abraham crossing Canaan with his flock, Jacob tending to Laban's sheep, and, perhaps most famous, Psalm 23: "The Lord is my shepherd, I shall not want. . . . Thy rod and thy staff, they comfort me." For me the stick's appeal stemmed mostly from the book of Exodus. During Moses' trials in Egypt, his stick is a veritable magic wand, turning into a python and splitting the Red Sea. Yet, in a touch of biblical irony, the stick is also Moses' downfall. He is forbidden entry into the Land of Israel because, in his impatience to draw water from a rock, he ignores God's instructions to speak to the rock and instead strikes it with his stick.

Hans, still seated, picked up his stick and laid it across his lap. It was about seven feet long and the diameter of a quarter. The dark brown wood was covered with small knobs where branches had been whittled away. A second small piece of wood, shaped in an "L," was nailed to the top like an upside-down coat hook. The hook, Hans explained, was for catching a sheep's leg. The stick had a flat top, as opposed to the curved crook on a traditional shepherd's stick, so that Hans has something to lean on during long stretches of standing.

While I was admiring the stick, a backpacked and bearded hiker in knee-high socks strolled by. He looked at the sheep for a moment, then asked Hans how many there were (this is the first question most people ask Hans when they encounter the flock). Hans answered him, and the man then asked why the flock had stopped in this field. Hans offered another brief answer, then turned to me. "People think that a shepherd only walks with the sheep," he said, "but I must always calculate how much grass they have eaten and where there is good grass and where they are allowed to walk. A farmer will look at me and say, 'What does this crazy shepherd do, moving his sheep in so many different directions?' or 'Why does this shepherd not move his sheep such long time?' He does not understand that sometimes the sheep are in the shade and not eating good, or that I must go very far to find place to put the sheep for the night, or that later in the day there will not be good food and so I must keep them in one place and make sure they have just right amount of protein. This is one reason my singing is important for the sheep. It keeps them calm so they will stay and eat when they are not happy with the grass."

At our first interview in Brooklyn, Hans had told me that his singing could inspire the sheep to keep moving during strenuous uphill climbs. I pointed out the seeming contradiction.

"It can be both," he said. "It depends on the rhythm. If I want the sheep should move quickly, I must sing with fast rhythm like this." Hans began making loud, throaty, yodeling noises. "It makes like a magnet, a little bit like when you walk yourself and you sing and this keeps you moving. The sheep hear the fast music, and they stop thinking and looking. But if I sing slow songs, then this can help them relax and not be distracted so they will eat good."

If only Bashy could have increased the number of latkes I consumed by singing, I thought, she too would have devoted all of her spare time to memorizing Yiddish folk songs.

In the afternoon I was given the responsibility of running back every half hour and driving the van up to the flock so that we would not have to retrieve it at the end of the day. The key to this job is to avoid running over the lambs, which seem to have little regard for massive motor vehicles despite their terror of my petting them. I didn't particularly like driving duty, as it took me out of my shepherding groove, but I didn't want to complain. Later it began to pour, and I came to appreciate my time in the van. The rain cleared in an hour, and not long after, we reached a clearing where Kati had already set up the netted orange fence. When the sheep were safely enclosed, we jumped back in the van, and I capped off my triumphant first day of shepherding by slamming the van's door on my stick.

We drove back to Manfred and Lore's for the night. Kati was already there, but she didn't want to sleep in the same room as Hans. She and Wolfi set up a tent near the sheep. Andi slept in the living room, and Hans and I were given the spare bedroom, which had two beds lined head to head against the wall.

Unpacking our clothes, Hans and I struck up a conversation about Yiddish, and I mentioned my family's tendency to add *gezunt* to the end of every other verb. Hans lit up. He had never heard most of the expressions I mentioned. He practiced saying *shlof gezunt* (sleep in health) a few times, then paused, the smile still stuck on his face. "I would like to continue our conversation," he said, "but first I want to express, I am happy at last to find a point where you reacted with personal details. I mean, you are doing a good job as journalist, but I like to see people outside of their job. When you ask questions, it gives me some imagination about you, and I'm also interested in you personally. I don't want that it is only one-way route."

I was embarrassed, but I understood. Hans had been revealing himself to me all day, and I had offered very little in return. On the one hand, I wanted to be a good journalist and keep my emotional distance from my subject; but on the other hand, my trip was more than a search for objective truths. I already had an emotional stake in Hans's story. I decided right then that I was going to stop playing reporter all the time and let my relationship with Hans develop more naturally.

What I hadn't decided right then was that it was okay for Hans to lean over my bed and make sure that I was tucked in snugly, as he did some ten minutes later. I pictured Mike

Wallace being tucked in by one of his subjects after a long day of reporting. I felt ridiculous, but I was touched.

When it was clear that I was nice and cozy, Hans climbed into his own bed, and we began to chat with the lights out, like a couple of third graders at a sleepover party. I told Hans a little bit about my life in New York, and he began to tell me about his childhood, half of which was spent fighting Nazism, the other half fighting almost everything else.

# Five

# Burden on My Soul, Very Heavy

On October 23, 1943, eleven years before Hans was born, his mother, Rosa, came home from a long day of work and sat down on the living room couch. Her feet hurt from standing all day at the factory, where, along with hundreds of other young Viennese women, she labored to make medical bandages for Nazi troops and horses. A staunch Communist, Rosa had been fighting fascism from the time she was old enough to hand out pamphlets. She had taken the job only to ensure that the Nazis wouldn't send her off to work in Germany.

Before Rosa, then twenty-three years old, could take her shoes off, she heard a loud knock. Rosa opened the front door to a tall man dressed in plain work clothes. The man, who spoke German with a French accent, told Rosa that he was a French Communist with information for Rosa's father, Johann. Rosa had no reason to distrust the man. Her entire family was involved in the Communist underground, and another Communist from France had arrived only the week before.

Rosa invited the man to sit and wait until Johann came home from work. Rosa sat down across from him. An hour passed. The man took a gold cigarette case out of his pocket and removed a cigarette. Now Rosa was suspicious. No good Communist would have carried a gold cigarette case.

Another hour passed before Johann arrived home and led the man to the back of the small apartment to speak with him. As they spoke, Rosa glanced out of the window. The streets were pitch-black so that Allied bombers would not be able to locate their targets, but Rosa could make out three cars parked across the street. The cars, an unusual sight in her neighborhood, made her nervous. She checked them again and again but saw no one inside. Then she spotted the red glow of a cigarette above a steering wheel.

Now the man made sense. He was a Gestapo agent. The cars were his escort. Rosa took a deep breath and walked to the back room. She poked her head in and told the man that there were cars waiting for him. The game was up, but the man stayed in character, insisting that the Gestapo cars were there to capture him. He jumped up from his chair and asked to be let out the back door.

Rosa and Johann thought that the scare was over, at least for the time being. They sat down and tried to think of what to do next. Fifteen minutes later a small team of Gestapo agents burst through the front door. They kicked Johann in the stomach and handcuffed him.

Rosa raced to her bedroom and pulled out her black dress of mourning. A fellow Communist and Nazi hater, Rosa's husband had been killed fighting on the Russian front in 1941. "My husband died fighting for the Nazis," she screamed, holding up the garment. One of the Gestapo agents ripped the dress out of Rosa's hands.

Johann and Rosa were taken away to the Gestapo's Vienna headquarters at the Hotel Metropol—a luxury hotel with upholstered doors to ensure privacy—where they were tortured for days. Among their tormentors was the same agent who had sat in the family's living room pretending to be a Communist. The agents demanded names of other Communists, but Rosa remained silent. After three days of beatings and listening to her father's moans from an adjacent room, Rosa began to wonder how much longer she could hold out before giving the Gestapo agents the information they wanted. Later that night, as an agent marched her up a set of stairs, she saw her chance. She took small steps. "Walk faster," the agent ordered from the stair below her. At the third floor Rosa looked down and decided she was not high enough. She continued to climb slowly. When she reached the landing of the fourth floor, she raced to her right and dived headfirst over the banister. The agent caught her feet. Rosa, upside down, grabbed the bottom of the banister with her hands and kicked furiously. One shoe came off in the agent's hand. With her free leg, Rosa landed a blow to the agent's head. The second shoe came off in his other hand.

Rosa survived the fall, but her psychological wounds never healed. More than fifteen years later, when Hans was a young boy, he would awake in the night to the sound of his mother screaming from nightmares about her torturers. Rosa would sleep in the living room so as not to wake her husband, but Hans would wake up and run to his mother's side to calm her. Rosa would be lying in a pool of sweat, and Hans would hold her hand and ask what was wrong. They would talk into the night, Rosa sparing no details about her trials at the hands of the Gestapo.

At the time, Rosa was editing and writing for a Communist women's newspaper. Sometimes she covered the trials of former Nazis, and in the process she witnessed firsthand one of the great scandals of postwar Europe. In 1945, under heavy pressure from the occupying Allied forces, the new provisional Austrian government passed anti-Nazi legislation, and extrajudiciary courts known as *Volksgerichte*, or "people's court," were set up. (The judges were hard to find because so many had been Nazis.) Nazi voting rights were restricted, and former members of the party were prevented from holding a wide array of government positions. Thousands of low-ranking Nazis were tried and convicted by the *Volksgerichte*. Forty-three were sentenced to death and thirty executed.

But in 1948 a general amnesty restored voting rights to all former Nazis, excluding a handful of the worst offenders. And in their efforts to win the former Nazi votes, Austria's two major political camps, the socialists and the Christian conservatives, managed to bring the prosecution of war criminals to a near halt. Thousands of the early convictions of the *Volksgerichte* were overturned, so that by 1955, when the Allies left and Austria became an independent state, there were hardly any Nazis still in jail. Working on a 1997 study of 350 Nazi criminals who had been sentenced to more than ten years in jail (a number of them to life imprisonment) in the late 1940s, the Austrian scholar Winfried R. Garscha was astonished to discover that only 7 were still in jail by 1955.

In 1957 a new amnesty law managed to wipe out a huge number of the remaining pending cases, many against high-ranking Nazis. The proceedings might have come to a complete halt if not for the Eichmann trial in Jerusalem in 1961, which put Austria under international pressure to prosecute more of its Nazi perpetrators. The Federal Minister of the Interior set up a special police unit to collect evidence against Austrian war criminals. They investigated some 5,000 individuals who had been previously reported and found extensive evidence, often of involvement in mass murders. Only eighteen of these men went to jail.

For Austria's political observers in the '50s and '60s, the same scene repeated itself again and again. Murderers walked free because of lack of evidence, or because they were merely following orders—an excuse that had been deemed legally irrelevant until the 1957 amnesty. In 1960, Rosa discovered that the same Gestapo agent who had shown up at her door that night in 1943 and then ruthlessly tortured her was living in a big house in Vienna and sang in the choir of a nearby church. Rosa turned to the police, who told her that unless she could clearly pin a murder on the accused, she should give up.

And so it's no wonder, then, that when Hans began to tell me about his childhood in the '50s and '60s, his first words were "Growing up in this country, I always felt as if I was among enemies." I was lying on my back staring up into the darkness. Hans's words floated to me through the chilly mountain air in the room. "I think these nights spent comforting my mother from nightmares took away my childhood from me," Hans said. "I was very interested and always asked questions from very little, and she answered me the truth. Those nights are burden on my soul, very heavy, but I think this is central to my life, and it influences all of my activities."

In 1963, when Hans was nine, Rosa put together an exhibition on Nazi crimes for the Communist Party. At a time when almost no one in the country would speak about what the Austrian Nazis had done, Hans was busy helping his mother lay out booklets with the stacks of photos of Nazi victims she had tracked down. Among the photos, Hans found pictures of children his own age. "These photos made very strong impression on me," Hans said. "I would sit for long time and only stare into the eyes of all the Polish and Russian and Jewish children that had been killed."

While Rosa was teaching Hans about Austria's Nazi past, his father, Georg, was training his son to be a good Communist. Georg worked for the Communist Party's central organ until he was expelled in 1957 for his anti-Stalinism, and he was known for his orthodox Marxism. "My father was one of these Communists who treated it almost like religion," Hans said. "If you had question, he would go to his bookshelf and say, 'Marx says this' or 'Lenin says this.' "

Hans became so adept at parroting Georg's opinions that the other party members began calling him "the Little

Breuer." By age ten Hans was composing his own political pamphlets on Vietnam and nuclear arms. At eleven he sold the most raffle tickets in his Communist Youth group and was rewarded with a weeklong trip to an international camp in the Soviet Union. "People thought that I would be just like my father," Hans told me. "But I have always been different from my father. For him the world is in order. Even with the Holocaust, it changed nothing. He says, 'I am Austrian, this is my home. This is my culture.' For me it is not like this. I was born after the Holocaust, knowing my mother had been tortured, so everything was broken for me. In the center for me was big broken thing. No home. No nation. No feelings of security. Only criminals. And with background like this and all of the things my parents taught me, I had either to be scared and not move at all or to become radical."

The conversation drifted off. Hans said that we should get some sleep. Then he changed his mind and said he needed to tell me about a Yiddish song called "Ofyn Veg Shteyt a Boym" ("By the Road Stands a Tree"). Hans sang a few mournful lines in a voice just above a whisper. The song is about a little boy who is crippled by his mother's love:

> By the road stands a bent tree;
> All the birds have flown away,
> And the tree stands deserted.
>
> I say to momma—"Listen,
> If you don't stand in my way,

Then, one—two,
I'll quickly become a bird.

. . . . . . . . . . . .

I lift my wing, but it's hard . . .
Too many things, too many things
Has momma put on her weak little fledgling.

I look sadly into my momma's eyes;
Her love did not allow me to become a bird.

Hans told me that when he first heard the song, he
couldn't understand it. But it nevertheless had had a powerful impact on him. He would play the tape over and over,
until he and Kati were able to sing the melody together.
When he came across the lyrics a year later, he was blown
away. He felt the song spoke directly to his sorrows, and it
sparked a new Freudian curiosity about all the psychological
troubles he'd experienced as an adult. "I discovered that so
many of my insecure behaviors with Kati go back to these
nights I spent in my mother's bed," Hans said. "My mother
would hold me, and even now I cannot sleep good unless
someone holds my hand or my foot in the night."

I told Hans I understood. The conversation drifted off
again until we were both quiet. I could hear that Hans was
asleep by the heaviness of his breathing.

⌒

In most ways it was striking how different Hans's childhood
had been from mine. At an age when Hans was planning
protests with his father, I still wasn't allowed to leave Bashy's
side in the women's department at JCPenney. And yet I felt

as though I could relate to what Hans had just told me—not to the historical drama or to the anger or to the way Hans had acted out, but to the burden on his soul, to the profound sense, even from a very young age, that nothing was stable or secure. And like Hans, I trace my feeling back to what happened to my mother.

I spent so much time with Bashy during my childhood because my mother wasn't around. She was diagnosed with an unusually progressive case of multiple sclerosis when I was three, and I have only a few isolated memories of her before she lost her ability to walk and talk and think clearly. She died the morning after my fourteenth birthday.

Despite the devastating loss, I was a mostly happy kid, too young to fully absorb the tragedy. Even moments that I now realize others must have found heartbreaking—the times my maternal grandmother, still struggling to accept what had happened to her daughter, would have me sit on my mother's lap and tell her stories about my life I knew she couldn't comprehend, or the times my grandparents took us fishing and made me hold a pole in my mom's useless hands as she sat in a lawn chair gazing blankly out over the lake—seemed entirely ordinary to me.

Then I hit adolescence, and the veil of childhood slipped off. The lesson of my mother's illness finally hit me: There were no guarantees. My father could be taken away just like my mother had been. Almost overnight the central question in my life switched from *Where's the next basketball game?* to *Is my father alive and safe?*

If my father went out in the evening, I would stay awake until he came home, peering out the window every time a car passed in the hopes that it would be our 1980 beige Honda

Accord. Each car that didn't turn in to our driveway was a new blow. One night when I was twelve and we were in New York, my father went out at 10:00 P.M. to make copies. He said he would be back in fifteen minutes. Twenty minutes later he still hadn't returned, and I could already feel the change in my breathing. After an hour I was nauseous. I sat by the window picturing a cab barreling into my father's legs, a mugger's knife slicing through his side. By midnight I couldn't take it anymore. I went out into the streets to look for him. My father found me, walking along Broadway, my face ghost white. He took me to a therapist, but what could she say? My logic was tight. Without my father, in the center was a big broken thing.

# Six

# *Punschkrapferl
in My Pants*

I awoke at 9:30 to find myself alone in Manfred and Lore's guest bedroom. I was still overwhelmed by my new surroundings and still a little jet-lagged. I stumbled out of bed and into the kitchen. Hans and Andi were eating brown bread and thick hunks of cheese at the wooden breakfast table. Lore pointed me to the table with a *"bitte."*

"You slept good?" Hans asked. He was still groggy. His hair stuck out in every direction.

"Yes," I said.

"So you are ready for the mountain?" Andi asked with a giggle. Now that he was no longer shouting at the sheep, I noticed his voice was changing.

"I guess," I said. I liked that Andi was warming up to

me, but I didn't see why it was so ridiculous for an American city kid to be doing a little hiking. What exactly did these people take me for? I got my answer a moment later when I sat down at the table and cut myself a very uneven slice of bread from the round loaf. Andi laughed.

"You don't eat bread like this in America," he said. I wasn't sure if it was a question or a pronouncement.

"Sure, we eat all kinds of bread," I said.

"I mean with cuts," Andi said. "You don't have to make the cuts in your bread."

"Oh," I said, happy to have an excuse for my lack of co-ordination. "Yes, in America it is usually already cut." My life in Manhattan was seemingly as strange to Andi as his life as a lamb herder was to me.

I poured milk into the mug of coffee Lore had placed in front of me and spread an unidentified red jam over my misshapen slice of bread. Hans informed me that the mountain we would cross that day is the biggest mountain he faces throughout his annual trek. He did not mention that it would be covered with snow at the top, or that we would be subjected to several hours of freezing rain and wind, or that no one intended to bring a bottle of water.

A few minutes into the breakfast Manfred showed up in jeans and mud-caked galoshes, which he removed and left by the door. In the morning light I noticed the distinguished wrinkles on his square face. Manfred spoke to Hans in German, and Hans translated. "Manfred would like to know about New York," he said. "Do you like it there?"

"I love it. We have every type of person you can imagine," I said, then wondered why I'd chosen to mention New

York's diversity at that moment. Hans translated. We made small talk for several more minutes until a white van pulled into the driveway.

Manfred mumbled something to Hans. "This is sweets truck," Hans said. "Manfred says you should pick out whatever you like. He will buy for you."

My first thought: *This beautiful home in the Alps already seems like paradise, and now, to top it off, they have doughnut trucks that drive right up to the door.* My second thought: *Is Manfred being so kind to me because he suspects I'm a Jew?* Maybe he was just an extremely nice guy, I thought. But maybe I was the only Jew he'd ever met other than Hans, and the warmth I was feeling from him was really just the awkward manifestation of his guilt. For that matter, maybe Lore, who was now busy doing my laundry, didn't give everybody the constant *bitte* treatment.

I picked out a small squarish pastry with red frosting over a chocolaty middle and brought it back to the table. Hans told me that there is an old joke that this dessert, *Punschkrapferl,* is like the Social-Democratic Party of Austria: red, as in socialist, on the outside; brown, as in fascist, on the inside—a reference to the Party's quiet incorporation of thousands of former Nazis into its ranks after the war. I put the *Punschkrapferl* down and had my first genuinely crazy moment of the trip (unless you count the semen-on-the-backpack incident): I found myself not wanting to eat a dessert with Nazi fillings. I looked at Manfred, then back down at the *Punschkrapferl.* The only plan I could think of was to stuff the *Punschkrapferl* into my pants when no one was looking and then pronounce it delicious. But then I didn't particularly want a Nazi dessert in my pants either.

I glanced at Manfred again, and he smiled. I ate the *Punschkrapferl*.

After climbing into my overalls all by myself and packing a small lunch of bread, cheese, and cherry tomatoes, I joined Hans and Andi for the drive out to the mountain, where Kati and Wolfi had already begun the day's trek with the sheep. We parked the van at the base of the mountain, took out our sticks, and began the upward march. Andi bounded ahead, leaving Hans and me alone. The sheep were nowhere in sight.

It looked like it might rain again. I wore a blue raincoat tied around my waist and Wolfi's small, multicolored child's backpack, which said ADVANCE SYSTEM in big letters on the pocket. Hans wore his red and beige rain suit with navy patches on the shoulders and knees. The sportiness of the rain suit seemed an odd contrast to Hans's hat, and I pointed this out.

Hans laughed. "Yes, but this is special hat," he said, removing the hat from his head so I could get a better look. "The wool is not knitted or weaved. It has no structure, just one piece—like if you work clay." Hans shot me a self-satisfied look. "This hat holds for three generations," he said.

I glanced at Hans, and his eyes gave me permission to feel the hat. "To make this hat," Hans continued, "there is an old wooden machine. It has a long string on a stick. The stick is fixed in the upper part of the room, and the craftsman makes *bong bong bong*. He never touches the wool with his fingers, so it will all be the same structure." I imagined someone playing a harp, wool magically appearing in the air with each pluck. Hans handed me the hat. It weighed a good three to four pounds. A thin cord, used to carry the hat around the neck when it's not needed on the head, now dangled from opposite sides of the slightly upturned brim. Hans usually keeps the cord tucked into the hat. "There's only one person in all of Austria who makes these hats," Hans added. "He lives in East Tirol, and he learned this job in Hungary."

Austria's last wandering shepherd was apparently walking around in the hat of Austria's last gigantic hatmaker.

"So you met this man?" I asked.

"Yes, yes," Hans said. "But he did not let me look at his old wooden machine. It is family secret."

Now I was really impressed. A hat made by a mystery machine that goes *bong bong bong.* "So what do you call this kind of hat?" I asked.

Hans thought for a moment. "Felt," he said.

Hats like Hans's may be hard to come by these days, but they are believed to be the first brimmed hats ever invented and have been worn by travelers and shepherds for thousands of years. Known to the ancient Greeks as the *petasos,* the hat protects not only from the elements, but also from pesky bugs that circle around the brim, a safe distance from the wearer's face. I have yet to get to the bottom of the wooden machine that goes *bong bong bong,* but it is true that old felt makers like to keep the tools of their trade a secret.

As Hans spent several more minutes describing how he waterproofs his hat annually with lanolin (the grease from sheep's wool), I felt a jolt of jealousy. I was allowed to carry a stick, but only one person got to wear the big floppy hat.

Hans eventually put the hat back on his head, then bent

over and picked a bright red flower from a small green shrub. "This is *Almrausch*," he said, explaining that the flower has become a symbol for the Alps.

After having been tucked into bed the previous evening, I hadn't thought there was room on my trip for further emasculation. Then Hans stuck the *Almrausch* into a small airhole at the top of my hat.

"Thanks," I said. At the time I thought that I at least had a special Alpine treasure in my hat, but I now know that *Almrausch* is slang for *Alpenrose*—also known as a rhododendron.

We continued along slowly. As I walked, I tried to keep my head down so I wouldn't stumble over the pumpkin-sized boulders. Unlike the green pastures of the day before, the mountain had only scattered patches of vegetation. The sky was all clouds.

Hans can talk, uninterrupted, for a solid hour, and the morning's lecture was on the wonders of life in the Alps. Hans's obsession with the Alps and old Alpine culture is second only to his obsession with Yiddish. He talks about the superiority of Alpine cheese and milk as though he were running his own dairy up in the mountains. He talks about Alpine plants and trees as though he were describing the vegetation in the Garden of Eden. I was beginning to suspect that Hans became a "wandering" shepherd not because he feared a dry summer, but because he needed an excuse to get to the Alps.

I was enjoying Hans's enthusiasm, but I also remembered that in our first interview in Brooklyn, he had told me that he associates the Austrian countryside with fascism and anti-Semitism and that when he meets people in the mountains, they often look at him with cold eyes, aware that he is not one of them.

I pointed out the contradiction, and Hans quickly agreed. "You must understand, one reason I sing in Yiddish is that I cannot sing the old folk songs in German," he said. "This is real tension for me. Our national culture was destroyed by the Nazis. Not just in mountains, but all over. Only very conservative people would sing these old songs. But even as child, I had a strong emotional link to this old culture of the *Alm* [Alpine summer pasture]. Most Austrians—and not just Austrians, but also southern Germans and all the nations or ethnicities that are living around these mountains—are looking to them with lots of positive emotion. There is a very big sympathy for this old culture of moving with the animals to the mountains in summer and collecting berries and making firewood and coming down to the valley again in the autumn."

At the heart of Hans's attachment to the Alps is the *Alm*. Generally high in the mountains, above the timberlines, the *Alm* is a treeless green expanse (think *Heidi*) that is a bit like an oasis in the desert for grazing animals in search of fresh summer grass. Shepherds have been leading their flocks up the mountains to the *Alm*s for thousands of years, and Hans loves the idea that he is a living part of this dying tradition. It's the one sense in which his love of both Yiddish and old Alpine culture doesn't seem a contradiction at all. Yiddish and shepherding are relics of another time. And as I observed the great pride Hans took in both, I couldn't help but think that he sees himself, if only half-consciously, as a hero for keeping alive what others have left to die.

About halfway up the mountain we entered a thick fog. Hans, whom I could now barely see, said the sheep were nearby. I wasn't sure if he had arranged for Kati to leave the flock at a certain spot or if he had some way of sensing the sheep's presence. Then I spotted Andi lying on his back on top of a large rock.

There were no animals in sight. "What happened to the sheep?" I asked.

"They are over there eating." Hans pointed, but I couldn't see anything through the fog. "It is okay," Hans said. "The dog watches them."

Hans sat down and rested for a moment. I was extremely thirsty, but, to my amazement, no one had brought along water. I didn't want to sound wimpy, but I was beginning to feel slightly faint, and I wanted nothing less than to end the afternoon on my hands and knees vomiting.

I found a seat on a smooth rock and sucked the juice out of my cherry tomatoes. The sky was now dark gray, and a light drizzle had begun to fall. I rested and wondered if the thin air at high altitudes might kill brain cells, until Hans belted out "Hey, Tsigelech" in the distance. I looked up to see him leading the sheep back from their grazing patch, directly toward me. As the flock approached, Hans made a sharp turn before a large rock and headed upward, so that I had the chance to see the wet and matted sheep row by row as they made it over the small incline and then broke right. The fog created the illusion of sheep emerging from the sky, a heavenly entourage of snouty faces and matted wool. It was the stuff of dreams, or at least the stuff of our imagery of

dreams. I sat mesmerized as Hans and Andi continued along, Hans moving up the mountain and Andi and the dog forcing the stragglers back into line.

From that point on, the climb went from vaguely to obscenely strenuous. The wind began to whip my face, and the drizzle turned into a hard rain. I hurried to catch up to Andi, but I soon found myself falling farther and farther behind, unable to keep up with even the infant lambs that were literally wobbling up the mountain.

As I inched my way to the summit, the wind grew stronger and we began to encounter large pockets of snow and increasingly steep inclines. I fell even farther behind, until I could hardly see Andi's stick in the distance. No one seemed to notice that I was no longer around. I imagined Hans and Andi sharing a beer years later and thinking back to the American journalist who disappeared on the mountain. *He was a nice guy,* Andi would say. *But you should have seen the way he cut his bread.*

When I finally made it to the top, there was hardly any pleasure in the triumph. I was exhausted, and the view was entirely obscured by the fog. I'm not sure what happened to Andi, but I ended up sitting next to Hans, crouched in a small stone structure that had apparently been set up by shepherds or cattle herders long ago for just this purpose. The stones were only about waist high and there was no roof, but by hunkering down, we were able to stay out of the wind. While I sucked on a few remaining tomatoes and wondered how the hell I had ended up in this situation, Hans broke out into another chorus of the Yiddish song about the tailor preparing for the holidays. The song concludes with the tailor wondering if there will be any good food left over when the holiday is over, and I found myself empathizing with his dietary concerns.

Even as the freezing rain pounded our hats, Hans spoke admiringly of this small stone structure. After all, it was a part of the great Alpine culture! Soon he was back on his Alpine kick, telling me how early music may have emerged out of the instruments used by ancient herders to call their animals in the mountains. The Alpine history lesson ended with Hans standing up and running a few steps downhill with his stick dragging behind him. "This is origins of skiing," he said, laughing loudly.

Cold and grumpy, I laughed in spite of myself. I put on

Wolfi's multicolored backpack and began the descent. At the bottom of the mountain Kati and Wolfi were waiting on a rock. It was clear that she and Hans had a carefully arranged schedule, presumably designed by Kati to minimize her time with Hans; but from my perspective, Kati appeared to just pop in and out of our journey like a mischievous mountain sprite sent by the gods to play with Hans's mind.

It was decided that Hans and I would take the van to buy groceries, including more salt for the sheep, while Kati and the boys finished the day's shepherding duties. When we all met again at a field that had been chosen for the sheep's evening residence, Kati and Andi were visibly angry. They had been waiting for us for more than an hour. Kati and Hans had a brief argument, and then Kati drove off in her white Jeep.

"Kati tells me that Mohrle [the dog on duty] went a little bit crazy and attacked one of the sheep," Hans said to me. He was as mad as I had ever heard him. "I always tell her she makes too much pressure on this dog to move the sheep quickly, but she does not want to hear this."

The sheep was now missing and presumed dead. Back in the van Andi made the mistake of asking what had taken us so long. Hans's response to the question lasted a good half hour. Occasionally switching from German to English (for my benefit), Hans lectured Andi on money and responsibility. "This dentist of Kati's likes to take them out to dinner every night," Hans said, turning to me in the backseat, "so now they don't understand why I have to buy groceries. They think everyone should be reech." As Hans went on and on about the dentist spoiling his sons and filling their heads with "wrong ideas," I began to feel embarrassed for all of us. Hans couldn't stop himself. It was a side of him I hadn't seen before. He didn't seem in full control, and I wondered if this was part of the reason Kati hadn't always been so eager to sleep with him over the years.

I was relieved when we pulled up at our new lodgings, a beautiful two-story farmhouse set against a steep slope of tall grasses. It was getting dark, but it was still light enough for me to see the large white barn next to the house and the huge toolshed off to the side.

"You know," Hans said, sitting down on the back bumper of the van and yanking off his mud-covered boots, "this farmer who lives here is the best at cutting the grass."

"Cutting the grass?" I was digging through my backpack for a dry shirt.

"Yes, you know, with the sharp tool that they use."

"Lawn mower?"

"No, no, with the stick and the knife."

"Scythe?"

"Yes, yes. What is the word?"

"Scythe."

"Yes. Sye. This man is best in world with sye."

"What do you mean, 'best in world'?"

"He is the fastest. Faster than even tractor."

I was intrigued. "How do you know he's the fastest?"

"He won first place in the championships." Hans took off his pants and pulled on a new pair.

"Championships?"

"Yes, this is very big activity in countryside. People come from all over. I don't remember exactly, but I think he did more than one square meter a second."

I don't know if scything more than a square meter a second would have meant much to me out of context, but now I was a genuinely excited. I was about to meet the world's greatest scyther.

Hans knocked on the door of the house, but no one answered.

"This is not a problem," Hans said. "I have *Schlafsäcke* [sleeping bags] in the van, and we can go up to the little room there." Hans pointed to the toolshed. The door was open, and I could see at least a dozen scythes hanging from the walls. This sleeping arrangement didn't sound particularly pleasant, but I was hungry and tired, and so I went up to the little room in the attic of the shed and helped Andi clear away the nail-studded two-by-fours on the floor. Once we had changed out of our wet clothes and put down our sleeping bags, I thought the day was done. Then Hans announced that we would now go to the train station to pick up his girlfriend.

As we drove to the train station in the nearest town, Wolfi, who spoke almost no English, tried his hand at a little rapping. Again and again he barked out, "Come, my lady, come come, my lady, you're my sugarfly sweetheart baby"— lines from a song we had heard on the radio earlier in the day. I liked listening to his German-accented rapping, but Hans and Andi seemed less amused.

Christine was waiting for us under a lamppost at the train station. She had long, straight red hair and large red-rimmed glasses. Her face was full and radiant, and before she spoke a word, I sensed her kindness. She and Hans embraced. Hans made a brief introduction, and then we were off to dinner. As Hans and Christine and Wolfi chatted in the front seat, Andi and I played chess in the back. I lost badly, but after serious consideration I've decided not to add this defeat, nor the ones to come later that evening, to my list of emasculations.

Hans pulled up in front of a small Turkish kebab restaurant in a nearby town called Egal. The drab restaurant was covered mostly with unframed posters that looked like they came from Turkey's national tourism office. There were also several posters of scantily clad women on motorcycles. Christine's presence lifted everyone's mood, and the tension between Hans and Andi evaporated. We sat down in the empty restaurant and ordered our kebabs, or "kebaps," as they were called in this establishment. After we discussed the appropriate spelling of "kebab" for some time (even the guy behind the counter wasn't sure), Hans told me that Turkish kebab shops are common in the countryside, run by Turkish immigrants who are not so well liked in these areas.

As I finished my specially made meatless kebab, we laughed for a bit about my performance on the mountain, and Christine shared some of her own low points as a novice lamb herder. I learned over that dinner that Austrians know little, if anything, about *The Sound of Music*. Christine had heard of it, but there seemed to be no understanding of why Americans are so taken with the Von Trapps, and I wasn't able to offer any insight on the subject.

After dinner we headed over to an establishment that seemed to be part bar, part arcade. Teenage girls in tight shirts laughed and danced with one another by the bar. Seedy-looking men with mustaches and unbuttoned collars sat smoking at the tables. We headed to the foosball table, where Andi and I played on a team against Hans and Christine. Andi was unbelievably good at making miniature plastic men connected to metal poles play soccer, and our strategy quickly became for me to leave my players with their feet in the air so that I wouldn't accidentally block Andi's shots. Foosball, I would later find out, is an important part of the Breuer family story. Kati and the boys are passionate about the game, and it has directly impacted their love lives: Kati got to know the dentist over the foosball table, and Günter is currently involved with one of the top female foosball players in Austria.

The evening wore on. We played more foosball, laughing the whole time. Then Hans and Christine retreated to a table. I spotted them kissing as I played table hockey against Wolfi and began to have the strange and warm sensation that we were one happy, if dysfunctional, family: the shepherd, his mistress, the young lamb herders, and the journalist—all of us wandering together.

# Seven

# The Sheep Were Jews

When we arrived back at the home of the world's greatest scyther late that evening, I was delighted to discover that the scyther and his family had returned and left the front door open. This meant that I would not be sleeping in a *Schlafsäcke* in a loft above a dozen scythes, one of which, I would later learn, happens to be the biggest scythe in the world, made especially for our host. The prospect of sleeping so close to the scythes was an unwelcome reminder of the pins and thumbtacks on my old Ziggy bulletin board. One night when I was six or seven, it occurred to me that were an intruder to enter my room while I slept, I had more or less laid out an entire arsenal of weapons for him to use against me. From that night on, my Ziggy bulletin board remained pinless. I'm happy to say that I no longer worry about pins and thumbtacks in my bedroom, but scythes aren't exactly pins. They're sticks attached to boomerang-shaped swords that seem designed for efficient decapitation. And it's impossible to look at one without thinking of the grim reaper.

Later, when I mentioned my association of the scythe with death, Hans seemed genuinely offended. "In countryside we do not think like this," he said. "This is very valuable tool."

*Death*, I thought. Everywhere I turned there was death. The scythes, the dog attacking the sheep, my hypochondria, and, of course, the real death, the Holocaust. I felt especially ashamed that my obsession with the murder of Europe's Jews could coincide with my hypochondria. The seriousness of my thoughts about the Holocaust should have overwhelmed my neuroses, should have shocked me into a state of gratitude for my health and relatively comfortable life. But then, my neuroses are not easily overwhelmed. If there is one thing in this world I would not bet against, it's the ability of my deepest fears to withstand an onslaught of perspective.

Inside the house, the lights were off. Hans guided me up three flights of varnished wooden stairs to the attic, where I would be bunking with Wolfi. In addition to two twin beds, our room had a strange bedlike contraption with straps and bars along the sides. It was either a medical instrument or a medieval torture device.

*Death*, I thought, and crawled onto my sheetless bed.

"Som, you muust to breakfast now!" Wolfi called out the next morning. On my way downstairs, I noticed a wooden engraving of a man holding a scythe by its two handles, the thick blade pointing to the scyther's own ankle. Farther along the wall was a group portrait of about twenty smiling men all wearing lederhosen that strapped across the chest, feathered, green hunting hats, and kneesocks.

In the white-tiled kitchen, bathed in morning light, the world's greatest scyther sat drinking orange juice. He had short brown hair and massive shoulders. He had blue eyes and a veined tree stump for a neck. His forearms were thick and meaty enough to leave a cannibal salivating. When he stood up, I saw that he was at least six foot four and thick all around. He was, I realized, the Austrian Shaquille O'Neal, the "Shaq Daddy" of the Alps. Hans, who looked like a child next to the scyther, introduced me.

His name was Gottfried. I shook his enormous right hand, and then he was gone, off to the barn to tend to the cattle. Christine was getting ready, and Andi and Wolfi were playing Nintendo with another boy in the family. This left me, Hans, the scyther's tall blond wife, and one of the family's two young sons in the kitchen. Hans noted that the little boy, who was five years old, had one prosthetic foot. I didn't think much of it then, but later, when I saw scything in action, the blade sweeping across the earth, I couldn't help but wonder about that foot.

The tall blond wife brought

me coffee with Alpine milk. In the background I could hear the ding of metal against metal.

"This is the father of Gottfried," Hans said. "What you hear is the *Dengeln*."

I nodded, assuming Hans meant "dinging."

"You know this, *Dengeln*? He hits the 'sye' with small hammer to make sharp."

"Oh," I said, sipping my coffee.

"He does this always. He is best in the world."

I put down my coffee. "They have competitions for sharpening the scythes?"

"Yes, yes," Hans said, as though it was a silly question.

After breakfast Hans escorted me to the entrance of the barn, where Gottfried's father, Fritz, sat on a wooden stump, a miniature hammer in his right hand, a two-foot scythe blade spread across his lap—not the sort of item I would have wanted near my genitals. The smell of cattle shit swept through the mountain air. Fritz wore an oversized bright blue baseball cap. He was red-faced and stout and fleshy, his belly just one more slope in the hilly landscape. Upon being introduced to me, Fritz laughed and broke into a raspy German.

I tried to convey my lack of understanding with an awkward flailing of my arms, but Fritz kept on going. He was immensely likable, with a manic goofiness that brought to mind Curly of the Three Stooges.

"He speaks very old dialect of German, more similar to Yiddish," Hans said. "I like it very much. Perhaps later he and his son will sing for you."

Fritz was still smiling at me.

"Now he will show you *Dengeln*," Hans said. Fritz took

a sharp whetstone out of an animal-horn-turned-water-holder attached to his right rubber boot and began to smooth over the spots he had just hammered. Then he carefully pounded the blade for another twenty seconds and repeated the smoothing.

"How long have you been interested in *Dengeln*?" I asked, not entirely sure what I was talking about. (I now know that *dengeln* is the thinning of the *Dengel*, the eighth-of-an-inch-wide metal strip at the scythe's edge. It's a bit like jewelry making, more about skill than strength.)

Hans translated for both of us: "I started to scythe at eight and to *dengeln* at twelve," Fritz said, his eyes still focused on the blade. "My father was ill, and I had to do the scything when he could not."

"And you were the world champion?"

"Yes."

Fritz took a few more whacks at the scythe with his hammer, then explained how a *Dengeln* competition works. Five men sound the *Dengel* for half an hour, then a judge examines the blade with a magnifying glass to see if the metal has chipped in any place. The judges also test the blades "in special ways" with their fingernails. The metal "should not have waves going up and down, but be spread evenly."

I could have happily spent the afternoon watching Fritz pounding and smoothing metal, but the sheep had a big day of walking and eating ahead of them, and it was time to get dressed. Manfred had been kind enough to lend me his boots, and with the rainstorms seemingly over, I was able to leave my overalls in the car. More significant, when Hans, Christine, Andi, Wolfi, one of the scyther's young sons, and I arrived at the sheep's evening lodgings to release them from the fence, Hans handed me a new hat, a leathery Panama Jack getup. Was this Hans's way of telling me I was no longer a novice lamb herder? Was this like getting a new belt in karate? The new hat wasn't exactly Hans's felt crown, but I'd be lying if I said I wasn't pleased with this sudden reevaluation of my headwear.

The sheep were milling about near the edges of the netted orange fence, anxious to get going. Hans opened a section of the fence and began to lead them out with a long, echoing *"Koooooooooomm, koooooooooomm."*

If my outfit was a bit more glamorous that morning, the work was decidedly less so. Christine, Andi, and I were left with the job of pulling the fence posts up out of a muddy field, which in itself would not have been so bad had the sheep not left a minefield of shit in their wake. Andi went off by himself, while Christine and I worked as a team. I pulled the fence posts out of the ground and handed them to Christine for bundling and tying.

After a few minutes of work, my pants were covered in mud and sheep droppings up to the knee. I looked down and then up at Christine. "This is real shit work," I said.

Christine liked this line, and we began to chat as we worked. I learned that she was a high school teacher in Vienna and had recently received a degree in psychoanalysis. She and Hans had met after a Yiddish concert Hans gave to a group of Austrian students at another high school. Christine liked Hans's singing, and just by staring at him, she could tell he was a good man, if a bit lost. She identified with the sadness in Hans's eyes. A day later Hans was moving some of his things into her flat. Two days later she met *die Mama* and *den Papa* Breuer.

That was about four months earlier, and this was only Christine's third time working with the sheep. She said she liked to think of the work as meditation and to synchronize her breathing with her movement. Her English was smoother than Hans's, but, unlike Hans, who will happily make up usages when necessary, Christine grew flustered when she couldn't find a word, her face reddening, her eyes turning to the sky for help.

"Your friends must think it's strange that you've become a shepherdess on the weekends?" I noted.

"*Ja,*" Christine said, smiling, "but they are used to me doing crazy things." I liked Christine right away. She seemed smart and sweet, and she had an explosive, body-shaking laugh. Almost every time I pulled a fence post cleanly from the earth, she would nod and give me a "*Ja, ja,* this is goot."

Walking to the van, each of us with two fence bundles in our arms, I asked Christine if it bothered her that Hans still worked with Kati all the time.

"It is not easy for me," Christine said as she tossed the fences onto the smaller trailer attached to the back of the van. "They were together many years. For now I prefer not to see Kati. She is a nice woman, but I know they are together when they go with the sheep from the Danube day and night, and sometimes they are growing emotionally and sexually close, and this hurts me very much."

I felt for her. Hans's decision to continue shepherding with Kati was crazy. It was making both Christine and him, and no doubt Kati and the dentist, miserable. I thought back to the women I had hurt in the months before my trip and felt a wave of shame and guilt. The real problem with love, I thought, is that it's got nothing to do with morality.

Later Christine told me that during the war the Nazis had used the basement of her school as a prison. Part of the prison has now been turned into a small museum, and the school has been inviting former Jewish students who were exiled during the war to come and visit.

"You must come and see," Christine said. "Perhaps you will speak to my students?"

I pictured myself standing in front of a group of rowdy Austrian teens, spitballs moistening on the tips of their tongues: *Hi. I'm a Jew from New York. Any questions?*

"Um . . . I'll think about it," I said.

By the time the entire fence was bundled and stacked on the trailer, Hans was already far ahead with the sheep. I realized that the hat is only one of the perks of being the shepherd. You also get out of fence duty.

For the rest of the morning Christine and I took turns driving the van and helping the boys with the lamb herding. At one point Wolfi and Gottfried's son joined me in the van, and the three of us inched along the road watching the sheep and listening to terrible rap songs on an Austrian radio station. Hans was leading the sheep through a small residential area, and I began to see some of the appeal of being the only wandering shepherd in a country. Packs of little children chased us down the streets. Mothers stood on their doorsteps to watch. One old woman handed us ice-cream bars as we made our way past her home. The flock might just as well have been Michael Jackson's limo driving by.

Hans was too far ahead for me to see his face, but I already knew him well enough to know that he loved this attention. This was payback time for all those lonely hours in the wilderness, payback for the all the years of living in a cramped trailer. To the extent that Hans's shepherding was a romantic fantasy, the fantasy was coming true before my eyes.

But Hans was also working extremely hard. Leading 625 sheep through a residential area is a lot trickier than leading them through the mountains. As soon as his sheep stroll into town, the wandering shepherd has to be extremely vigilant of cars. But he also faces an even greater dilemma: preventing a huge flock of sheep from snacking on people's lawns and flowers.

The great sheep-snacking dilemma was first tackled in medieval Germany and England when Saxon farms and intensive agriculture arose in Europe. The Saxon estates were huge self-contained plots, complete with orchards, woods, and crop fields, and the farming system relied upon some patches of land remaining unplanted each season. These fallow fields, usually adjacent to crop fields, were an ideal food source for the sheep in the late summer and spring. But there was a catch. The only things missing from the self-contained Saxon estates were fences, meaning that if the sheep had been allowed to graze freely, the crop fields would have ended up as little more than a light morning brunch.

To overcome the absence of fences, the shepherds of the time devised a technique that Hans calls "near herding." The common English term is "tending," but it is also sometimes called the "living fence" technique, because the dogs' obsessive patrolling of the flock's borders cages the sheep in just like a fence. Shepherds had already been using dogs for driving and gathering their flocks for centuries, but the living fence technique transformed shepherding from a lifestyle into a science. Never before had the dogs been able to maintain a large flock with such precision; never before could a sheep be expected to behave itself while standing just a few feet from a field of turnips. This shepherding revolution never caught on in most of the world because there was no need to bring the sheep so close to forbidden fields, and now very few people outside of Germany know how to make a fence come to life.

I discovered the effectiveness of living fences later that afternoon as I attempted to make my way to Hans along the side of the flock. Before I was halfway to Hans, a car appeared on the horizon, and I found myself standing along the border between the sheep and the car lane with Mohrle, the very same Mohrle who had attacked a sheep the previous day, racing toward me with bloodlust in her eyes. With no other option, I skirted into the middle of the pack.

To my surprise, the sheep seemed unfazed by my presence, and when I looked up at Hans, he too appeared unbothered by the sudden turn of events. And so I walked along with the others, the denim of my jeans brushing against the wool of their coats with each step. Despite my discovery that swarming flies are an integral part of flock culture, I enjoyed being part of the gang. Wherever we were headed, we were headed there together. After several minutes of internal debate, I let out a soft, self-conscious *baaah* and looked around to see if the sheep had taken notice. They hadn't.

Then, standing in a sea of wool, my imagination took off. I envisioned the sheep as European Jews being led to the slaughter. Indeed, for the lambs, I thought, it was a genuine death march. And as I watched Mohrle harass and bite the sheep on their hind legs, I couldn't help but think of her as the Nazi guard. This wasn't entirely my craziness. The comparison of Europe's Jews to sheep walking to the slaughter is well known, the preferred metaphor of some Zionists who saw the unwillingness of most of the Nazis' victims to fight back as a sign of weakness. I find the comparison offensive, but the image didn't fade quickly. For those next few minutes the sheep were Jews.

I grew so lost in thought that I became oblivious to the hundreds of sheep and flies around me. When the traffic cleared, the sheep spread out across the road like a stream opening into a river, and I made my way to Hans, the bottom of my stick scraping the pavement.

# Eight

# Vienna, 1968

In the spring of 1969, Hans decided he could no longer live at home. He threw a few shirts into his rucksack, grabbed his toothbrush, and headed out. His father stood blocking the door.

"Get out of my way," Hans said. He was fifteen. He had hair down to his shoulders and black-framed glasses and a jacket with a white peace symbol painted on the back. Georg didn't move.

"This isn't a jail," Hans shouted. "You can't keep me here."

Georg didn't move.

Hans took a step toward his father. Georg was thin and wiry but strong. He looked down at his son. "You're not going anywhere," he said.

It wasn't the first standoff between Hans and his parents. A month before, Hans's mother, Rosa, had blocked him, not with her body, but with a pleading voice. She asked Hans to go with her to see a psychologist before he moved out, and Hans agreed because he had never been able to disobey his mother. The doctor asked Hans to solve simple puzzles. Hans sat with his arms crossed; Georg and Rosa stood behind him.

"If you could be any animal, what animal would you be?" the doctor asked. The room had the institutional feel of a hospital. The doctor had thick owlish eyebrows.

"I'd be a fly so I wouldn't have to live in this corrupt world for another day," Hans said.

The doctor took Georg and Rosa aside and told them they should let Hans go. "You can't hold a child like him," the doctor said.

But Georg wasn't ready to let go, wasn't ready to accept what he already knew: that he had lost Hans to the older teenagers in his Communist Youth group—the Viennese '68ers.

The 1968 movement in Austria was relatively small, but the youth revolts that shook Paris and Berlin and Berkeley also took place among the New Left in Vienna, and Hans and his friends in Section 6 of the Communist Youth were the most radical members of the scene. Like the New Left around the world, the Viennese '68ers were convinced that fascism and Nazism had never gone away, only put on a disguise and found new victims. As the journalist Paul Berman explains in A Tale of Two Utopias, the new fascists were the capitalists and imperialists; the victims, whomever they oppressed: the Algerians, the Vietcong, the Palestinians.

But there was one crucial difference between the Viennese '68ers and their counterparts. For most young leftists to look at western European social democracies and see Nazism in disguise took an act of political imagination, layers of often convoluted philosophy that a series of radical French thinkers were more than ready to supply. But Hans and his friends didn't need the French ideologues to see Nazis in every sphere of society. They understood that their government was rife with former Nazis. They understood that all the postwar trials of Austrian Nazis had come to nothing and that the "former" Nazis were the judges, lawyers, doctors, and teachers they encountered every day.

What they couldn't understand was how their parents, the same Communist parents who had gone underground to fight the Nazis when they were teenagers, didn't want them to go to battle for the cause. "We were criticizing very hard the Austrian Communists," Hans said. "They were engaged in strong arguments: pro-Czechoslovakia and contra, who is Stalinist, who is not. We were against this. We said this is not important. We cannot use all our force in ideological discussions. We must fight here in Austria and set up concrete things."

Near the end of 1968, Section 6 of the Communist Youth cut its ties to the party and changed its name to Spartakus Kampfbund der Jugend (Spartacus Youth Action Group). A dozen of the most active members of the group moved into a large apartment in the Sixth District of Vienna and turned it into a commune. They slept on the floor, often all in one room, and ate noodles. Whatever money they scraped together from shoveling snow or hitting up their parents was immediately turned over to the collective. In their

spare time they trained in hand-to-hand combat and cam-
paigned against Austria's youth reformatories—known to
Hans and his friends as "youth concentration camps." They
hid escapees from the reformatories and chained themselves
to landmarks around Vienna. Once the group broke into a
popular live television show with a young escapee who
shouted out his story to all of Austria.

Hans continued to live at home until 1969, but he spent
as much time as he could with Spartakus. "I thought to be a
part of this group was the only useful thing to do in this country," Hans told me. "The logical consequence of all these
teachings I got from my parents could only lead to a more
radical point of view, but my father was against this radical-
ism and so we had big conflict."

And so Hans had decided to move out. He took another
step toward his father until they were face-to-face "I'm not
going to fight you," he said. Georg didn't answer and he
didn't move.

"Please, Hansie," Rosa said, "stop this." She was watching the standoff from the kitchen table. Without releasing his
gaze from his father's eyes, Hans walked backward to the
first-floor window, then jumped out into a new life.

# Nine

## Jew City

"Som, you must come," Wolfi called.

I jolted up from my nap. Downstairs the whole shepherding gang was assembled, and we were off for an early-
evening ice-cream trip to the nearby town where we had
picked up Christine from the train station. I hadn't known
the night before that the name of this town was Judenburg, or
"Jews' Castle."

Judenburg, population 10,000, is one of the oldest cities
in Austria. An important commercial center in the Middle
Ages, the city lies on a series of descending plateaus and is
now known for its happening winter sports scene. "Jews'
Castle" was not a city name I had expected to encounter in
the Austrian countryside, or anywhere else for that matter.
In fact, there are a handful of old villages in Austria with

"Juden" in the name. These "Juden" towns began to appear in the tenth and eleventh centuries, when Italian Jewish merchants set up trading posts across the Alps. Jews at the time played an important role in long-distance commerce largely because they were banned from almost all other professions. In the following centuries the privilege of trading was also taken away, and most Jews turned to moneylending, the remaining work available to them.

Not much is known about the early history of Judenburg. The first mention of Jewish traders in Austria is from a document of C.E. 906, signed by forty merchants, among them a "Ysac" and a "Salaman." The first mention of the city is found in a document from 1075. Although *Burg* means "castle" in German, the name comes from *Burgus*, which at the time meant a trading place near or in front of a castle. Judenburg was founded near the castle of Eppenstein, which still lies some ten kilometers from the old city center and trading area.

The Jews of Judenburg suffered the same fate as other Styrian Jews during the Middle Ages. They were sometimes protected by the local authorities who valued their role as financiers and sometimes attacked and murdered by raging mobs. At the turn of the fifteenth century bands of *Judenhauer* (Jew beaters) began attacking Jews across Styria, threatening to burn down the city of any ruler who tried to stop them. One of the worst anti-Semitic riots in Judenburg took place in 1312, when word spread that the Jews were planning to murder all the Christians in town on the night of Christmas—a Jewish girl who had fallen in love with a Christian boy had supposedly revealed the plan. In response, the Christians set about murdering those Jews of Judenburg who hadn't already fled for their lives. Legend has it that when a Jewish massacre took place in Judenburg, the last Jew caught was strangled with a chain at the city gate, known as *Judenthörl*, or "Jews' gate."

This gate still exists, and we sat at an outdoor table not far from it and ordered double-scoop ice-cream cones. Across from us a round fountain sprayed water in small arcs. Wolfi continued to rap his "Sugarfly Baby" song, Andi and I played chess on a small magnetic board, and Hans and Christine made eyes at each other.

Judenburg was quaint, with well-kept plazas, lightly colored two-story buildings, and windowsill flower beds to spare. At some point during my trip I realized that almost all Austrian towns feel like a collection of life-sized dollhouses, albeit ones in which the dolls eat an enormous amount of schnitzel.

"So how do the people here feel about living in a town named after the Jews?" I asked Hans while Andi pondered his next chess move. I was surprised that with all the anti-Semitism in the area over the centuries, no one had gotten around to changing the name of the city.

"They make up stories," Hans said. "It's incredible. Watch, you will see."

When our ice creams arrived, Hans turned to the waiter. "Do you know why this city is called Judenburg?" Hans asked. The waiter, a young man with moussed blond hair, looked at him, startled.

"It's a long story," he said, setting our order on the table.

"*Ja?*" Hans said, eyebrows raised.

"There is an old castle, and the duke who lived there, his

named was similar to 'Juden,' and when you change the name a little bit . . ."

Hans nodded politely. "So it doesn't come from Jews?"

"I don't think so," the waiter said. "I don't know." His eyes twitched. He was clearly uncomfortable, and I felt sorry for him.

Hans spent the next few minutes telling the waiter about the Jewish traders who had founded his city.

The waiter listened patiently, nodding along to Hans's history lesson. When he left, Hans turned to me. "We will bring the sheep through Judenburg in the next weeks," he said. "We will ask the people about their city."

Hans then continued his lecture for a bit, noting that the Jews were involved in the trade of lavender plants, which grow in the mountains. He also mentioned that the city's official symbol, or coat of arms, is the head of a Jew.

I found this last detail hard to believe, but Hans pointed to a city sign a few yards away, and sure enough, there was what appeared to be a profile of a bearded Jew wearing the large lampshade-style hat that Jews were often forced to don in medieval Europe so that they wouldn't be mistaken for Christians. (The hats were often worn together with yellow badges similar to those the Nazis would later force Jews to pin to their sleeves.) The Jew's head appears on the city's buses and on its official webpage, even on the local soccer team's logo.

"It's really creepy," I said, my eyes still fixed on the Jew's head.

"It's incredible," Hans said, his arm now around Christine. Hans told me that he had given a concert in Judenburg but that it took him more than a year of haggling and a call from a local music teacher to convince city officials to let him perform. The cultural expert from the city council specifically told Hans he shouldn't make a link between his songs and the city's name.

"This is typical," Hans said. "Not just here, but all over Austria. Before my performances I always ask that the person from the city who introduces me should say why I sing in Yiddish, and out of twenty, maybe one agrees. They don't say no. They say, 'This is not my function. It's better you do it yourself.' "

The waiter bravely returned and asked if we would like anything else. I feared Hans would go after him again.

"*Kaffee, bitte,*" I said.

The waiter looked at me confused, and Christine instructed me to order a Melange—half coffee, half milk with a frothy top. In the following weeks I was to drink dozens of Melanges because it was the only item I knew how to order.

When the waiter brought my drink, Hans returned to his lecture on the medieval lavender trade. I caught Christine's eyes with a "Here we go again" look, and she burst out laughing.

"What?" Hans said. "I can sometimes talk too much?"

We all laughed, and then Hans, smiling, turned to Christine. "Why do you laugh at me?" he asked.

"Because I love you," Christine said, then she leaned forward and kissed Hans on the mouth, leaving her lips against his for several seconds.

When we made it back to the scyther's house, Fritz was standing by the front door eating gummy worms. He dangled one in front of me, and I tried to fend him off without success. I went upstairs to go to sleep. Hans popped his head into my attic bedroom and said, "*Shlof gezunt, shtey uf gezunt.*"

The next day we hardly moved the sheep at all. Gottfried was happy to have them clear some of the grass he would otherwise have had to scythe, and the flock spent the day as a 625-headed lawn mower. *The world is their salad bar,* I thought. Hans, wearing an uncharacteristically nice sweater-vest over a button-down shirt, looked on and sang, his stick propped under his armpit for support.

Christine and Andi had gone ahead to set up the fence for the night. I milled around, watching the sheep and listening to Hans. Eventually I found a shit-free patch of grass and lay down and looked at the countryside and listened. The Austrian hills were alive with the sounds of bleating sheep and Yiddish music, and for at least a few minutes I felt at peace. I pictured a Hasidic Jew spinning atop a green hill, arms spread, like Julie Andrews in *The Sound of Music.* I couldn't understand most of the songs, but I got the important words: the *mama*s and the *tati*s, the *oy vey*s, the *chosen*s (grooms) and the *ḳalah*s (brides). I liked thinking about those medieval Jewish traders walking these same hills and speaking these same words. Yiddish had long ago disappeared from this part of the world, but it was there for a day, and I was a part of it.

I dozed off, but when I opened my eyes a few minutes

later, nothing had changed. Hans was still leaning on his stick, Churka was still eyeing the sheep as though they were terrorist suspects getting ready to board a plane.

A few feet to my right a lamb cried out for its mother.

"You want to hear a little Yiddish song I've written?" Hans asked.

"Of course," I said, somewhat surprised that Hans, who didn't speak very good Yiddish, was writing songs in the language.

Hans sang four melodic lines in the anguished voice of a cantor on Yom Kippur, then translated for me:

Play klezmer a tango, good without end
Play klezmer a tango, *oy vey iz mir.*
Play klezmer a tango, my heart is tired
Play klezmer a tango, play this song.

"Tango?" I said.

"Yes, in Canada I learned klezmer tango music is very warm now."

"Warm?"

"Yes, it is very popular."

"You mean hot?"

"Yes, hot."

I looked over at the flock. Several dozen sheep had gathered together in front of the dog.

"They are on strike," Hans said. "They would like very much to keep moving because they have already finished the best grass here. Some of them are eating, but the strong ones are saying, 'Oh, we can wait. We can wait.' " Hans used a ridiculous, cartoonish voice for the sheep, and I wondered if that was how he really imagined their personalities.

An hour later Hans said, "The strike is over. I am defeated." He called to Churka and walked to the front of the flock.

In the distance I saw Fritz scything near the house and went over for a firsthand look. Fritz wore an oversized baseball cap with a cow on it. He acknowledged my arrival with a nod and continued to work. I had imagined scything involving golflike swings at the grass, which is why, I suppose, it had struck me as so dangerous. Instead, Fritz bent over at the waist and dragged the scythe horizontally across the ground in swooping arcs.

Every minute or two Fritz would stop, pick up some freshly cut grass, and run it along the blade. Then he'd take out his whetstone, which he now kept in a little red holder on his back, and smooth the blade down. It seemed as though clearing the entire hill would have taken him all year, but Fritz was clearly much more interested in the sharpness of his scythe than in actually removing the grass.

I gestured to myself, as in, *How about I give it a try?* fully expecting the always jovial Fritz to let out a good laugh. But Fritz looked concerned as he handed me his tool. The scythe was heavy, and pulling it along the grass wasn't as easy as I had anticipated. Worried that I would hurt my back, I returned the scythe to Fritz, who was examining the work I had just done with a look of genuine disgust.

# Ten

# The Domesticated Life

Over the next week in the Alps, I learned that putting up a fence for the sheep on a slope sometimes requires placing large rocks at the bottom of the fence's netting so that the sheep can't sneak out underneath, and that Hans sees nothing unusual about asking a journalist who has come to interview him to haul large rocks on his shoulders, and that it doesn't feel so good to be standing next to a dog and to have someone say, "I am leaving, but do not worry, the dog is in charge," and that Hans once almost drowned in the process of smuggling a lamb into Austria from Germany by swimming across a river, and that when Hans made it across, a group of Austrian hunters in lederhosen discovered him naked on the bank of the river gasping for air with an exhausted lamb a few feet away, and that Hans thought Kati wore revealing tank tops just to torture him, and that just because you're a guest in the home of the world's greatest scyther doesn't mean his son is going to let you have the first turn on his Nintendo.

What I hadn't managed to learn about was Gottfried. Each night when we came back from the sheep, I would try to locate him, but Gottfried was never available.

Then, on what I had scheduled to be my last night in the Alps, my luck turned. The evening began at the kitchen table with Hans and Fritz, who had just finished his *dengeln* for the day. Hans told Fritz that I wanted to talk more about scything and Gottfried's records, and Fritz responded with a few "*ja*'s." Then he stood up and left the room, only to come back a minute later with a stack of papers, which turned out to be score sheets from Gottfried's various competitions. Fritz was all business as we looked over the score sheets. He turned the pages crisply, pointing to Gottfried's name atop every list. Apparently, the numbers revealed that Gottfried had managed to scythe more than one square meter per second in recent competitions.

"Does Gottfried practice a lot?" I asked.

Hans translated. "Always. He makes his practice and then gives it to the cows so they can eat."

"And do people ever get injured?"

"Very seldom. The participants control their tools well, so it is safe."

There was more shuffling of papers and an exchange between Hans and Fritz. Hans turned back to me. "In the next competition he expects Gottfried will do forty-nine square meters in thirty-two or thirty-three seconds."

I had no idea what the number meant. "Wow," I said.

Then Gottfried lumbered into the kitchen in a pointy green mountain hat and a long-sleeved cotton shirt. He glanced down at the papers in his father's hands.

"*Ich mähe 1.39 Quadratmeter in einer Sekunde* [I will cut 1.39 square meters in one second]," Gottfried said. Hans did the translating. Gottfried walked over to the kitchen counter to pick up a calculator. "Since long time I had vision that human with only hand tool can cut grass quicker than one square meter in one second. All the other scythers in Europe said this is utopia, but I did it. Now, when I am healthy, I will make forty-nine square meters in thirty-two seconds." Gottfried began punching numbers into the calculator. "This will make 1.5 square meter in one second," he said. He brought over the calculator to show me the number: 1.53125.

"Wow," I said. "How long is the blade of your scythe?"

"It is 1.4 meters [4 feet 7 inches]. This is biggest in world."

I nodded. Hans had his big shepherd's stick, and Gottfried had his enormous scythe. *Maybe I should start writing with one of those giant souvenir pencils*, I thought.

"You have heard of Falco?" Gottfried asked in English.

I had. In 1986, Falco had become the first Austrian to top the American pop charts with "Rock Me Amadeus."

"Amadeus Amadeus," I said.

Gottfried smiled.

Hans asked Gottfried if he and his father would sing for us.

Fritz looked a little embarrassed, but Hans encouraged him and he agreed. He walked over to the kitchen to grab a beer. "He must first wet his pipes," Hans said. Fritz returned with a beer for me as well. Then he and Gottfried belted out a shockingly good yodeling duet: *"Dingle Dengel donger dinger Dengel donger dinger dooo, yo de le he hoooo, yo de le he hooo."* Gottfried was a real virtuoso, his voice climbing higher with each yodeled syllable.

My enthusiasm was only slightly dimmed when I later played my tape from the evening for a German-speaking friend and discovered that Fritz and Gottfried had been singing a crude song about mountain girls, in which *dengeln*-ing was a thinly veiled metaphor for screwing.

For the next act Gottfried went solo, yodeling about a cuckoo bird: *"Cuckoo cuckoo cuck-el-le-eh-hoo, cuck-el-le-eh-hoo."*

I took a few swigs of beer and clapped when he finished.

"Do you sing?" Gottfried asked, growing more comfortable with his English.

"No," I said, then thought for a moment. "But I do rap."

Hans took a minute to translate "rap." "Yes, I would like to hear this," Gottfried said.

I took another swig of beer and broke into an old-school song about girls with big butts hanging on my jock.

No response. I considered apologizing. Then Hans, perhaps feeling a little bit left out, said that he too had something to sing. Hans broke out into a Yiddish song called "Zol Shoyn Kumen di Geule" ("Let the Redemption Come"). The tempo was upbeat, but Hans still managed to infuse the words with melancholy.

"Very fine," Gottfried said in English when Hans finished.

"The song says, 'Wake up, Messiah, from your little nap, your little dreaming after having dinner,'" Hans explained. "'Wake up, and we hope you will not wake up too late to come and save us.' " Hans paused and looked at the table. "For some it was too late."

When I arrived at breakfast the next morning, the changing of Hans's woman had taken place. Christine was gone, and Kati was sitting next to Wolfi at the table. I felt a certain loyalty to Christine by that point, and Kati's presence made me uncomfortable. We sat across from each other without trying to bridge our language gap.

I was headed to Vienna that night. I would stay with Christine and meet up with Hans in the city on the weekend—Kati would take over the flock. After packing my things and saying good-bye to Gottfried and Fritz, I caught up with Hans atop the hill behind the house. He was talking to Kati on his cell phone, even though she was only a hundred yards behind him at the back of the flock. It felt too early in the morning to hammer Hans with questions about his past, so I drifted along in silence and thought about cancer, which is what hypochondriacs do when we have nothing pressing on the agenda.

We were on our way to Judenburg, where Hans had to take the sheep in order to use the nearest bridge across the Mur River. We walked along a wooded path in the mountains until we reached a barbed-wire fence blocking our way. The entire flock came to a halt. Hans and Kati began to argue over how to proceed. Hans wanted to cut the fence and then, after the flock had passed, repair it with a wire kit he carried for just such occasions. Kati thought there was enough space for the sheep to squeeze through if someone held the wires apart. At a pause in the argument Hans pointed to the curls of barbed wire along the top of the fence. "This is why we no longer have the donkey," he said. "It was too hard to pass the fences." It was the first I had heard of the donkey.

"You see what these people do with their fences," Hans continued. "It makes me think of concentration camp." Hans rambled on about the Austrian landowning aristocrats and how they hate to let people on their property and how the only things they care about are money and hunting. Then he told me to take a photo of the barbed wire, as though it were evidence of the dark side of the Austrian character. I was running low on film and talked him out of it. "They use barbed wire everywhere," I said, in a rare moment of rational perspective.

Kati won the fence argument, and the sheep took turns, one by one squeezing between two strips of wire. "This is the difference between a wandering shepherd and others," Hans said, squatting and pulling up on the wire with a stick so that the sheep wouldn't get scratched as they made their way through. "Others see a fence and decide they cannot go there, but a shepherd must think about the best routes no matter where people have put fences. You have to look at the world very different." I remembered that the day before, Christine had talked about having walked through this same part of the country last year. Now that she was working as a shepherd, she said, she couldn't look at the landscape in the same way. Before she saw beauty in the mountains; now she saw beauty in a good patch of grass.

On the outskirts of Judenburg, groups of curious children appeared on the sidewalks. The sheep took over the road, and the line of cars behind us grew longer and longer, until it was hard not to feel the pressure of the interrupted lives. Later, in one of our only conversations, Kati found the English to tell me that the local radio station in Judenburg will sometimes announce that the sheep are in town so that people can avoid the traffic.

We made our way to the bridge. The sheep filled one lane of the road and the cars the other, so that the drivers, if only for a second, might have felt as though they too were a part of the flock or that the long line of cars was a gasoline-fueled flock of its own, with stop signs for a shepherd and honking horns for *hops*.

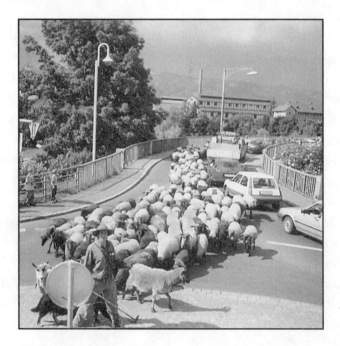

At the end of the bridge Hans and the sheep walked past a MCDONALD'S JUDENBURG sign. Two middle-aged women with tired eyes stood nearby, watching the sheep and smoking. Hans asked them if they knew why Judenburg was called Judenburg.

The first woman said that the name may have come from the Jews, but she quickly conceded when the second women said that, no, Judenburg comes from an old duke whose name was similar to "Juden." Hans smiled and began his history lesson. The women looked on confused, no doubt surprised to find themselves suddenly listening to a lecture on medieval Jewry from a wandering shepherd.

In a city park that afternoon, the flock stopped for a leisurely lunch. Hans sat down next to me on a bench.

"It feels weird to be in a city with the sheep," I said as I watched a lamb curl up for a nap under the shade of a water fountain.

"This is another reason I like being shepherd," Hans said. "As wandering shepherd, you have very special perspective. You see all different levels of society. First you walk by the fields of farmer, then through city, then along the banks of the river with fisherman, then you pass over the grounds of one of these aristocratic landowners, then you meet the people on the bicycle paths. You begin to understand how all these people live."

I liked this observation, but at the moment I was thinking not about the people, but about how the sheep lived. I was impressed by how independent they seemed as they spread out across the park. Why, I wondered for the first time, were they so willing to follow around a man in a big hat who cuts off their testicles and periodically slaughters them? The dogs were urging them along, but the system could work only if the sheep were willing to buy into it. Wouldn't the sheep be better off ignoring the shepherd?

Part of the answer, I've since learned, is that sheep are born to play follow the leader. Like other species that travel in herds, wild sheep usually have a flock leader that walks in front of the group and leads them to new pastures. The leader will most likely be an independent animal and among the dominant members of the group—although not necessarily the most dominant. In the eyes of the sheep, the shepherd is merely another member of the flock who has assumed this leadership position.

But the larger question of how sheep came to be so comfortable around man is really the question of how sheep first came to be domesticated some 10,000 years ago. The widely held understanding of animal domestication credits ancient man for capturing wild animals and breeding them into docile, cuddly versions of their unruly forebears. Wolves were too vicious, so we turned them into dogs. Wildcats were transformed into lovable kitties. Although I confess to not having put too much thought into the subject prior to my trip, I had always assumed that this was more or less how it happened.

The problem with this theory is that the fossil record reveals that sheep tended to hang around ancient man even before our ancestors were eating them in large numbers. In other words, rather than being captured, sheep were coming to us out of their own free sheep will. Also, humans have tried and failed to domesticate other species, which suggests that something outside of our control must have made sheep more amenable than, say, bears to domestication.

In the alternative theory, made popular by the science journalist Stephen Budiansky, domesticated animals evolved for the simple reason that the docile life was full of advantages for them. If this animal-centered view of domestication is right, Hans's sheep are following him, his singing notwithstanding, because the partnership between man and sheep turned out to be a pretty good deal for the sheep. Man got meat—wool came later; but the sheep got food, medical care, and protection.

According to this animal-centered theory, the story of sheep domestication goes something like this: Man started cultivating plants and staying in one general area. The sheep that were more curious and less fearful began to hang around these early human settlements and eat from the grain fields much like mice hang around our kitchens today. At some point man realized he could make good use of these tame sheep and began to herd them and eat them according to his own needs. But it was the sheep, at least those that didn't get eaten, that were arguably getting the better part of the deal. The numbers speak for themselves. There are more than a billion domesticated sheep today, while wild sheep are almost extinct.

For the animal-centered theory to work, there must have been a genetic mutation that led to the first docile sheep. And here's where the story of animal domestication becomes particularly strange. The mutation that separates domesticated animals from wild animals appears to lie in those genes that determine when the animal becomes an adult. Domesticated animals reach sexual maturity as adolescents and then simply never grow up to be wild. That is, in both appearance and behavior, domesticated animals are remarkably similar to the young of their wild progenitors. Adult dogs both look like juvenile wolves and exhibit the same submissive traits: They whine, roll over to expose their bellies, and, like all domesticated animals, are less fearful around other species. In sheep the best evidence for this permanent adolescence, known as "neoteny," is the large size of a domesticated ram's horns. Unlike wild rams, which stop growing their horns in adolescence, domesticated rams grow their horns throughout their lives.

Budiansky theorizes that the melting of vast glaciers that occurred around 8500 B.C.E., at the end of the geologic epoch known as the Pleistocene, would have provided an advantage to animals that exhibited juvenile curiosity. These animals would have been more likely to explore, and thus benefit from, the newly unfrozen frontiers. And because domesticated animals tend to reach sexual maturity at a younger age than their wild counterparts, they would have had the advantage of higher reproductive rates.

Put another way, the sheep were hanging around Hans because they were teenagers who had figured out how to exploit him for free food, like a nearsighted clerk at a 7-Eleven.

⌐‾‾‾

We ate dinner at a roadside restaurant that night. Hans and Kati argued the entire time. I played chess with Andi at the side of the table, thankful to have an excuse to ignore the tense conversation. With Christine, the group felt like a loving dysfunctional family. Now we just felt dysfunctional.

There were several teenagers sitting near us in slightly out-of-style hip-hop attire. Hans leaned over and asked them if they knew why Judenburg was called Judenburg. A plump girl in a sweat suit giggled. "Because of the *Juden*," she said. Her friend turned red and hit her in the arm. They both laughed. Then a blond-haired guy in an Adidas sun visor said, "Why is Knittelfeld called Knittelfeld? It's just a name. It doesn't mean anything." His agitation was obvious. Hans let it go.

On the way out Hans stopped by the bar and asked a mean-looking mustached man in shiny boots if he knew the origins of his city's name.

Without turning to face us, the man snarled, "Go read a history book." Hans gave me a knowing glance and we left.

At the Judenburg train station Hans told me for at least the third time how good it made him feel to be around someone like me who understood him. I felt suddenly nervous. I didn't yet feel as though I understood him. I still had a lot of questions, still needed to get to the bottom of his transition from radical teen to a wandering shepherd, still needed to figure out exactly how Yiddish had come into the picture.

"I'll see you in Vienna in a few days," Hans said.

"*Zay gezunt*," I said.

## Eleven

# The Shepherd
# in the Airport

The shepherd and I are wandering through Houston's Intercontinental Airport. We are waiting. Around us people are eating Cinnabons and talking about missed connections. Away from his sheep and without his stick, the shepherd seems uneasy. In the gift shop he drops a glass water globe. A miniature Alamo spills out.

"What's wrong?" I ask.

"I miss my wife," the shepherd says.

"I know," I say. "But there are lots of women here. Talk to them. They'll find your accent charming."

"I do not want other women," the shepherd says. "I want my wife."

"I'm sorry," I say. "Let's go to Burger King."

We go to Burger King. I order a fish sandwich and a

Dr Pepper. The shepherd orders a cheeseburger. When he is finished, he sings a Yiddish song about a lonely tailor under his breath.

Across from us, an attractive blond woman with hoop earrings is dipping fries into a small paper tub of ketchup.

"Just go talk to her," I say.

The shepherd gets up and sits down across from the woman.

She looks nervous. "I am shepherd from Austria," the shepherd says.

"I'm Darlene," the woman says. "I'm a cashier from Laredo."

"I am without my sheep," the shepherd says.

"I can see that," Darlene says. "Want a fry?"

The shepherd takes a fistful of fries. "My country is full of old fascists," he says. "People know what happened during the war but act as if they do not know because they want to believe this myth that Austria is veecteem."

"What's a fascist?"

"Someone who cares only for power."

Darlene laughs. "We got those here too."

"You are beautiful woman," the shepherd says. "Perhaps you would like to wander with me some hours?"

"You're sweet," Darlene says, "but I've got a plane to catch. You want the rest of my fries?"

The shepherd comes back to my table. We go on waiting. Days pass and our flight never arrives. The shepherd begins hitting on more and more women. After a month he has approached almost every female employee in the airport. It looks bleak. I eat more fish sandwiches and try not to worry.

One day I come back from the bathroom in Concourse C

and the shepherd is holding the hand of a glowing redheaded woman.

"This is Shayna," he says. "I found a woman who understands me very well and would like to be with me."

The shepherd and Shayna become an item. She wanders the airport's wide hallways with us and tells us stories about the outside world. The shepherd seems more relaxed. He observes the herding instincts in an immigration official's German shepherd. He tries his first Cinnabon and enjoys it.

We wait and wait. The sadness returns to the shepherd's eyes. "I miss my wife," he says.

"Forget your wife," I say. "She ran off with a dentist. Now you have Shayna."

"But I am not happy," the shepherd says.

"No one is happy," I say.

"You are too young to understand," the shepherd says.

But I do understand. The plane is not going to come because the shepherd isn't ready for it to come.

The next morning I board a flight to Toledo. The shepherd cries. I tell him everything is going to be okay, but I don't believe it.

# Twelve

# The Wandering Jew

The first sentence I ever read about Hans, in the Yugntruf e-mail, described him as "a wandering Jew." I didn't think much of the label at the time, but in the months prior to my trip just about everyone I spoke with made Wandering Jew asides, and I thought I had better figure out what they were talking about before I left for Austria. I don't remember when I first heard the expression "Wandering Jew," but I'd always assumed it was a playful reference to the Jewish Diaspora. The Jews didn't have a homeland, so they were roaming the earth as wandering Jews.

I had it all wrong. The Wandering Jew is a specific Jew, a legendary figure destined to walk the earth for eternity, or at least until Christ returns. Over the centuries the legend of the Wandering Jew has taken on countless variations in different countries, but the earliest written accounts from the thirteenth century go something like this: Jesus is walking through Jerusalem carrying his cross to Calvary when he stops to rest on the doorstep of a house along the road. Unhappy to find Jesus loitering on his property, the owner of the house shouts, "Walk faster!" In some accounts the man hits Jesus; in others it is only a verbal assault. Either way, Jesus is not amused and responds, "I go, but you will walk until I come again."

In the early versions of the legend, the Wandering Jew is a fairly affable character who spends much of his time doing good deeds. Even more impressive, he has an array of cool superpowers, including a knack for sniffing out hidden treasures and predicting the future. Sometimes he can make himself invisible. On rare occasions he heals the sick.

But over the centuries the Wandering Jew grew much less likable as he became the product of a distinctly anti-Semitic imagination. Whereas in the early versions of the legend he is depicted as an ordinary traveler dressed in plain friar's garb, by the seventeenth century he is lanky with flowing hair, bare feet, and beggar's rags. (In some descriptions he carries a staff.) Rather than making friends by revealing hidden treasures, he is now guilt-ridden and depressive, and his magic is thought to reveal his association with the Antichrist.

The most influential account of the legend, the *Kurtze Beschreibung* pamphlet, dates back to 1602 and identifies the Wandering Jew as a morose shoemaker named Ahasuerus with soles on his feet "the thickness of two fingers across." The *Kurtze Beschreibung* inspired countless imitations over the next centuries and turned the Wandering Jew into an international sensation. Soon Wandering Jew imposters were popping up across Europe, some of them swindlers, most seemingly just looking for a little attention.

In the eighteenth century the Wandering Jew began to make his way out of the strict confines of the anti-Semitic imagination and into a broader literary imagination. Reflecting the popular fascination with foreign travel at the time, different authors have the wandering Jew trekking across every part of the world. One French account has the Wandering Jew on the North Pole, where he finds himself trapped, his feet held to the earth by the magnetic force. (He escapes by sliding his feet along the ground until the force diminishes.) An English writer puts the Wandering Jew on the moon, where he is surprised to find the inhabitants made of metal and engaged in a brutal war. (The noise of the moon surgeons banging away at their injured brethren irritates the Wandering Jew, and he soon leaves to visit the planets.)

But though his adventures grew more fantastic, the Wandering Jew remained more folk legend than fully realized fictional character in these accounts. Few authors mentioned his inner life or described how he experienced his suffering. Then along came the Romantics with a new approach to the Wandering Jew. No longer was it sufficient to note that "none ever saw him laugh." The Romantics were interested in why the Wandering Jew wasn't laughing. What was it like to live forever, watching generation after generation die? What sort of psychological toll did endless isolation have on a man?

Over the course of the late eighteenth and nineteenth centuries few of the major English Romantics were able to resist at least a passing stab at these questions. Shelley alone wrote five separate works that relate to the legend, either directly or indirectly, including both "The Wandering Jew's Soliloquy" and *The Wandering Jew.* And it wasn't only the English poets who caught the Wandering Jew bug. Goethe wrote a number of fragments of what was to be a lengthy work on the Wandering Jew before giving up with the excuse that he didn't have time to study the background materials. Another German, Christian Schubart, wrote perhaps the most influential work on the Wandering Jew of the period. In Schubart's "Der ewige Jude" ("The Eternal Jew"), the Wandering Jew stands atop a mountain and rolls down the skulls of family members as he recalls the various ways he has tried to kill himself over the centuries.

It's easy to see why the Romantics were obsessed with the idea of an eternally Wandering Jew. Wandering is a romantic gesture, at once a rejection of the world and a search for something new. And what better metaphor than an eternal wanderer for the loneliness of the human experience, for the elusiveness of human connection? Then, to top it off, the guy's a Jew. The Jewish wanderer is the Romantic's dream come true, an outsider among the outsiders, a sufferer among the suffering.

I don't know how much of my own romanticizing of wandering and Jewishness had drawn me to Hans. Certainly from the beginning I was fascinated by the metaphorical possibilities of Hans's life. In his shepherding I saw the rejection of modern society in the aftermath of the Holocaust. In his Yiddish songs I inevitably listened for the millions of missing Yiddish voices that should have been singing along.

The problem is that metaphor obscures as easily as it illuminates. As I prepared to deepen my understanding of Hans in the days ahead by meeting with his friends and relatives, I wanted to see Hans less for what he represented and more for who he was.

At the same time, I knew that I would have to transcend my neuroses if I was ever going to be able to look at Austria as more than a cauldron of Jew hatred. Austria might be full of anti-Semites, I thought, but I'll never really know unless I step back and do some rational observing. If I was going to get Austria right, I was going to have to unlock Bashy's front door and give the goyim their say.

# Thirteen

## Meet the Mozarts

"Gut, Som, you made it," Christine greeted me, seemingly as surprised as I was that I had managed to find her apartment on the west side of Vienna. Christine lived in a prewar building with a dingy lobby and a wide spiraling staircase. Along the middle of each story was a row of wooden closets with toilets in them. "It was cheaper to build with toilets on outside," Hans would later explain.

Christine had a toilet inside of her apartment and a kitchen with curvy marble counters, bright yellow cabinets, and a poster of a Chinese man ferrying several women across murky waters. The kitchen opened onto Christine's bedroom, where she had a pyramid-shaped bookshelf. The modern touches, together with a dangling wind chime and a handful of well-placed candles, gave the apartment a distinctly New Agey feel, the feel of a place where one might meditate without irony.

The strangest part of the arrangement was the glass-paneled shower, which stood in the hallway for all to see, as though the architect had forgotten about it and stuck it where he could at the last moment. The shower became more than a passing curiosity when Christine handed me a towel and told me to go ahead.

I wasn't sure what to do. Was I supposed to get naked in this woman's hallway? I began to pace back and forth, soap in hand, until Christine popped her head in from the kitchen and, registering my concern, said that she would close the door and not come out.

I still wasn't thrilled with the situation, but I was dirty from shepherding and there was really no choice. As I stood in the shower—positioned in such a way that if Christine broke her promise and stepped out into the hall, she would not see my penis—it occurred to me that I was in an anti-Semitic country, in the home of a Gentile, hiding my circumcised penis. *So much for overcoming my neurotic imagination,* I thought.

The next morning I stuffed my not-so-compact green alarm clock into my pocket (I didn't have a watch) and began gathering my notebooks and blank tapes. It was only then that I realized I had no bag other than my large hiking backpack. Christine had already left for the day, and so I grabbed the only thing I could find—a plastic, black garbage bag—threw my notebooks and tape recorder in, and hurried into downtown Vienna for the first time.

When you emerge from the Stephansplatz subway station in central Vienna, the first thing you see is Stephans-

dom—St. Stephen's Cathedral—an enormous Gothic structure that dates back to the twelfth century. It has spires and
catacombs and all of the other things that make old European cathedrals so scary. It also has a multicolored, patterned roof, which—unfortunately, since it's the most visible
landmark in the city—calls to mind argyle socks.

The next thing you notice when you exit Vienna's subway, or U-bahn, are the handful of strolling teenagers
dressed as Mozart. Decked out in big white wigs, knee-
length frocks, and ruffled cuffs, the young Mozarts patrol the
plaza in front of Stephansdom like a royal guard. The worst
thing you can do in downtown Vienna is give the impression
that you're not a local because the moment you do, the
Mozarts will descend upon you, ask questions about your
musical interests, and then, regardless of your answer, try to
sell you tickets to the symphony.

That morning I had plans to meet with Leon Zelman,
the director and cofounder of Vienna's Jewish Welcome Service. Before my trip I had called the Jewish Welcome Service
and arranged an interview by announcing that I was a "journalist from New York"—a title I would use again and again
in the days ahead after discovering that it allowed me access
to almost anyone in the country.

The Jewish Welcome Service is located directly across
from Stephansdom, at the back of the offices of an Austrian
travel agency. As I waited for Zelman, I held my garbage
bag of notebooks behind my back, hoping that he wouldn't
spot it until it was too late to cancel the interview. My alarm
clock ticked against my thigh like a bomb waiting to go off.
Around me Austrian travel agents with blond ponytails
planned the vacations of their fellow countrymen.

I had no real idea who Zelman was or what I would ask him, but I was still determined to figure out if Austria was a Nazi country, and the Jewish Welcome Service seemed a natural place to start. Luckily for me, no one I met with seemed to mind or even notice that I lacked a good excuse to be conducting interviews with them. I was a journalist from New York. I wanted to talk. That was enough. In the weeks ahead I realized that no one was surprised that I wanted to sit down and talk about Nazis and Jörg Haider because that's all anyone was really talking about in Vienna that summer. It had been a little over a year since Haider's far-right Freedom Party had taken a stunning 27 percent of the vote and joined the government, and the country was still reverberating from the aftershocks of the election. Haider, whom *The New York Times* has called "the most famous Austrian since Hitler," was on the cover of the local newspapers almost every other day. The European Union had already called off its largely useless sanctions against Austria, but protests against the government were still taking place in downtown Vienna once a week. There was so much talk about Nazis that someone who didn't know better might have thought the war had ended years rather than decades earlier. The discussion was perhaps the one good thing that had emerged from the rise of the Freedom Party. It was no longer so easy to change the subject from Austria's past.

Zelman emerged from a back door wearing a sports coat and the type of oversized glasses that only the elderly can get away with. His eyebrows were bushy. His white hair had receded almost to the back of his head. We walked to a nearby café and took a seat outdoors under an umbrella. It was sweaty and crowded, and the streets were filled with tourists talking loudly about phone cards and streetcar fares. Zelman told me that he was a Holocaust survivor but that it was hard for him to discuss those years. When I left, he gave me a copy of his memoir, and I learned that he had grown up in a Polish shtetl, been transported first to the Łódź ghetto, later to Auschwitz, and then on to several other camps.

I had expected the head of the Jewish Welcome Service to be extremely critical of Haider, and he was. In a thick East European accent, Zelman spoke about the small distance between hateful rhetoric and violence and recalled a few of the many sympathetic comments Haider has made about Nazis over the years, such as his description in 1995 of Waffen-SS veterans as "decent men of good character."

But Zelman wasn't anti-Austrian. "I started here with nothing," he told me between sips of coffee. "No family. No language. Vienna gave me a chance to find a new identity. America didn't want me because I was sick at the time. I was too weak to travel to Israel. I wanted to go back to Poland, but there was no place for me to go. Vienna gave me a new belief in the future."

It was my first post-Hans interview, and already I began to feel like everything I knew was being turned on its head.

In the distance a heavyset tourist posed with his arm around a Mozart. "But what about all the anti-Semitism?" I asked.

"Yes," Zelman said, "but you must remember that Vienna has as rich a Jewish cultural history as any city in the world. There were so many great Jewish writers and musicians and doctors and so on. I feel a connection to that heritage. And from that heritage, I want to make a mission. I want to translate the Vienna of the past for a new generation so that they will understand what the Jews contributed to Viennese culture before 1938."

Zelman's plan to educate Austrians about Judaism made me think of Hans. Zelman was trying to teach Austrians about the Jewish past with his Jewish Welcome Service; Hans was trying to teach them with his singing. But neither of them, it occurred to me, had given up on the Austrian people.

Before we split up, Zelman asked me what had brought me to Austria, and I told him I had been following a shepherd who sings in Yiddish. There was a brief uncomfortable silence, and then I was off again, into the sea of tourists and overpriced souvenir shops selling Mozart rulers and "There are no kangaroos in Austria" T-shirts.

Later that afternoon I met with Dr. Thomas Frühwald. I had been given his name by Erich Loewy, an Austrian-born American professor of bioethics who had created a small stir in Austria a month earlier after accepting the city of Villach's award for achievements in the field of medicine. Villach is in Carinthia, the southern Austrian province where Haider was and still is governor, and Loewy chose to use his acceptance speech as an opportunity to speak out against the Freedom Party. "Anti-Semitism has entered the very fiber of [Austrian] society itself," Loewy bellowed to a packed auditorium. "It remains a part of the way we understand ourselves—something which for hundreds of years was promoted by the church and which will not be that quickly eradicated from the societal subconscious."

I had contacted Loewy after reading about the incident, but he was already back in the United States and recommended I speak with his friend Dr. Frühwald instead.

Frühwald and I met at Café Frauenhuber, the oldest

surviving coffeehouse in Vienna—Beethoven was once a regular. The café had vaulted ceilings and burgundy seats. The waiters wear formal attire and serious expressions, as though they are doing something much more important than serving strudel and flavorful coffees. On the front wall was a large wood-framed photo of a distinguished-looking man with a well-shorn beard and a white bow tie. Shortly after we sat down, Frühwald pointed out that the man in the photo was Karl Lueger, Vienna's mayor at the turn of the twentieth century, whose famously skillful use of anti-Semitism in politics inspired Hitler and helped pave the way for Nazi politicians in the decades ahead.

"And there's no shame in having his picture up?" I asked.

Frühwald laughed. "Why should this café be any different from the rest of the city? There's a statue of him not far from here, and the University of Vienna sits on Karl Lueger Ring."

Frühwald had come to the interview prepared, with more of a sense of what we were going to talk about than I had. After I ordered my Melange, he opened his briefcase and removed a newspaper article about a recent poll that had been conducted on Austrian feelings toward Jews. The poll had found that 45 percent of Austrians agreed with the statement that "Jews are exploiting the memory of the Nazi extermination of the Jews for their own purpose." In 1995 only 28 percent of Austrians agreed with the statement.

The increase may have reflected the recent skirmishes in Austria's decades-old battle with Jewish organizations and Western governments over restitution payments to Holocaust survivors, which Frühwald and I discussed for the next hour. Just eight months earlier the People's Party–Freedom Party coalition government had agreed to a settlement that would pay $415 million in reparations to Jewish slave laborers. It was still an insultingly small sum in the eyes of the Viennese Jewish community, and the move was seemingly a political ploy to undermine critics of the new government, but it was nevertheless another small step forward for Austria. Unlike postwar German leaders, who recognized the importance of reparations as a statement to the West that Germany was serious about denazification, Austrian leaders had spent the decades after the war repeatedly refusing to pay survivors or making insufficient offers under pressure from the United States and then failing to fully implement them.

And even as the Austrian government was systematically ignoring and undermining the issue of reparations to Jewish victims, it was bending over backward to accommodate the former Nazis who, as the argument went, had been the victims of a cruel campaign against them in the first few years after the war (when Austria briefly attempted denazification). "The victims of Nazi oppression are always told that the impoverished state lacks the means to pay," Austrian minister of education Felix Hurdes complained to his fellow cabinet ministers in 1950, "but where Nazis are concerned, the impoverished state always finds the money."

The reparations story is part of the same story as Austria's failure to imprison its Nazi criminals. Once voting rights had been restored to Austria's former Nazis in 1948, they immediately became a powerful voting bloc, and they had no interest in doling out money to Jews or handing over their stolen apartments, particularly in the first years after the war, when Austria experienced severe food and housing shortages. Not only did they not want to help the Jewish survivors, there was even a postwar protest outside of a camp for displaced persons, with angry Austrians falsely claiming that there was no money for them because the state was spending all its funds on the Jews. (In fact, Austria was paying nothing, leaving the American Jewish Joint Distribution Committee and the American army to address the needs of the survivors.) In 1946 a poll found that only 28 percent of Austrians were in favor of Jewish survivors returning to the country, with 46 percent against the idea. Taking its cue from the population, the Austrian government made no effort to entice its many Jewish emigrants back home.

But it wasn't just pressure from the Nazi voting bloc that kept Austria from paying for its crimes. Austrian leaders couldn't embrace the idea of reparations because to do so would have been to acknowledge guilt and thus to undermine the entire "victims rather than perpetrators" facade upon which postwar Austria was built. In the few instances where Austria was pressured to make a payment, the leaders were always careful to point out that they were doing so on moral rather than legal grounds. The government's line was always the same: If you have a complaint about the Nazis, take it to Germany. As the story goes, German chancellor Konrad Adenauer once remarked that if he heard Austrian diplomats try to shift all responsibility to Germany one more time, he was going to send Hitler's ashes home to the Austrian prime minister as a present.

It was six o'clock when I left Café Frauenhuber. I thought about shopping for a new bag, but most of the stores were closed. I sat down on a bench near a tired-looking blind man who was singing for money. It occurred to me that if I were to lose the napkin in my pocket with the directions to Christine's apartment, I would have nowhere to go. A wave of despair washed over me. After all, it's one thing to be alone in a new city and another to be alone in a new city after spending the day discussing its ties to the Third Reich.

I thought about calling Hans on his cell phone just to say hi, but I wanted to hold on to my last scraps of journalistic integrity. Then it hit me: You can never be truly alone in Vienna—there are always the Mozarts. I walked back to Stephansdom and was immediately approached by a white-wigged young man holding a clipboard and brochures. He asked me if I liked music. I told him that I did, and he told me that I was then sure to be very interested in an upcoming concert he had tickets for. I told him that I was a journalist and then asked him how long he had been selling tickets. He said for about a month. We chatted for a few minutes, and I learned that he was a newly arrived Bulgarian immigrant. "All of these people are from different countries," he said, pointing to the other costumed salespeople. (In addition to Mozarts, there were women in dirndls and other men seemingly dressed as generic eighteenth-century aristocrats.)

Before I left, the Mozart and I shook hands, and he told me that his name was Dimo.

I asked him why his name tag said ALEX.

"It's just easier to use that name here," Dimo said.

This name change bothered me, but Dimo didn't seem

to mind. We traded numbers, and he told me that I should come to his birthday party next week, that I would enjoy meeting his older sister. I thanked him, thought briefly about the likelihood of his sister being beautiful and wanting to make love to me, then headed back to the U-bahn.

# Fourteen

# Spartakus

For an athletic sixteen-year-old like Hans, climbing the scaffolding in the back of Vienna's Hotel Bristol wasn't hard. He was known as the best climber in Spartakus, which is why he had been assigned this mission. As Hans made his way across the roof of the hotel in the heart of downtown Vienna, the diplomats for the peace conference began filing in below. Hans knew there was a good chance he'd get arrested, but his comrades in Spartakus were counting on him. And this was what it meant to be a part of Spartakus, to take risks, to make a stand.

This is how a Spartakus newspaper from 1969 described the group:

> The name of the organization is Spartakus, but Spartakus is more than an organization. Spartakus means to have broken

away from everything, Spartakus means to be ready for anything.

We have set no limits. We stand outside this society, its laws, its petty considerations, compromises, comforts and lies. They know that, and hence they hate us.

This wasn't just rhetoric for Hans. His teenage revolt was not against his parents, but against an entire society. He continued to go to school after joining Spartakus, but it was hard to take his education seriously when he thought the teachers were fascists and the books full of lies. Hans told me that he had one teacher who would enter his classroom with a Nazi salute. Another teacher would shout commands like a military officer during gym class and would sometimes hit students with an iron rod. After witnessing one teacher slap a student, Hans dragged the student out of the school and led him to a nearby police station.

"I looked at the teachers as though they had tortured my mother," Hans told me. "Now when I tell Austrians about these teachers, they don't believe it. They don't want to realize that it's true. They forget that in the fifties and sixties, whenever there was professions where you needed a high school or university degree, we had a majority of horrible conservatives or fascists or National Socialists. All of the people who could very well survive Hitler were still around. The few others who were humanists or liberals or progressives did not come back after the war. They were killed or had emigrated or were in complete resignation—ill from the past and no longer able to teach. The result was that I was confronted with all these assholes."

Austria has a two-track high school system, and after a year Hans gave up on academics and opted for professional training. It didn't help. Even at a high school for graphic artists, Hans saw corruption everywhere. He talked back to the teachers, disrupted classes, and handed out flyers for protests. Before the year was over, he was not only kicked out of the school, but an order had also gone out that he should not be admitted to any public school in Austria.

"It was 1968, and I had respect in front of nobody other than these old fighters like my mother or grandfather," Hans said. "And there was this pressure that we should make a better world. It was a pressure we felt thinking of our parents, who suffered under the Nazis and fought against it. We thought about their courage to laugh in the face of death, to fight like my mother had, so that there would not be fascism again or such suffering, and we made emotional link, if you want, between our struggles and these struggles that took place in World War II."

Standing atop the hotel, Hans could see the security guards below with their guns in their hands. He looked out over Vienna, the city where he was born but had never felt at home. Then he walked over to the flagpole on the hotel's roof, pulled a blue and red Vietcong flag from his jacket pocket, and raised it high above the Austrian capital.

# Fifteen

# Jews for Haider

My next morning in Vienna made the previous one look smooth. Christine had moved me down the hall into the apartment of her friend, who was out of town. When my green alarm clock went off, I noticed that it was half an hour ahead of the nearly identical red alarm clock I had discovered in the apartment. Both of the clocks had shown the same time when I went to sleep, meaning that one of them was not working.

I had either an hour or half an hour before I had to leave to meet Peter Sichrovsky. I had read about Sichrovsky in the months prior to my trip and hadn't been able to get him entirely out of my mind since. Sichrovsky is an Austrian Jew, the child of Holocaust survivors (both of his grandmothers were killed at Auschwitz), and the author of several books on

Jewish themes. One of those books, *Strangers in Their Own Land,* is comprised of Sichrovsky's interviews with young Austrian and German Jews who recount the hardships of growing up "among the murderers."

Sichrovsky, at the time, was also the general secretary of Haider's Freedom Party. It made no sense, especially since Sichrovsky himself had denounced Haider in the past. Strangest of all, in an interview with *The Jerusalem Report,* Sichrovsky had readily acknowledged that Haider was using him as a Jew to deflect criticism from the Freedom Party.

Putting on my suit was out of the question, as I need a full forty-five minutes to tie, untie, and retie my tie until the knot no longer looks laughably gigantic. But I at least wanted my shoes to look respectable, so I took out the shoeshine kit I had purchased the day before and went to work on my sheep-feces-caked designer Australian boots. The polishing didn't go so well, and my boots ended up two different shades of brown and reeking of polish.

Since I had no way of knowing which of the two alarm clocks wasn't working, I shoved both of them into my pockets. At the time my only thought was that my pockets looked ridiculously overstuffed, but now it strikes me that the two clocks in my pockets keeping different time—and my not knowing which one was right—make a good metaphor for my state of mind that summer.

After several minutes in front of the mirror patting down the poof of my hair with wetted palms, I noticed that if I tilted my head just a bit to the right, it was possible, upon close inspection, to detect the tiny end of a hair peeking out from the abyss of my left nostril. I was not amused. Now, even if by some miracle I met a woman who wasn't bothered by my strangely bulging pockets, the nose hair would surely scare her off. I pinched and then yanked the hair, but it had its own agenda. After searching for and failing to find a pair of scissors, I began to panic.

Seeing no other obvious solution, I removed a key from my pocket and began to saw back and forth over the hair. I'm not sure how long this continued, but at some point I thought, *I've come to Vienna to explore anti-Semitism in the aftermath of the Holocaust, and I am standing in front of a mirror sawing my nose hair with a key.* I stopped in shame, then sniffled several times, hoping that the hair might somehow be sucked back in.

When I arrived at the address Sichrovsky's secretary had given me, the first thing I noticed were the letters "FPÖ" on the wall of the lobby. It was only then that I realized I was meeting Sichrovsky at the Vienna offices of the Freedom Party. Seeing the three big letters on the wall gave me a nervous chill. In my mind I had entered the lair of the enemy, and part of me wanted to turn around and run. Another part of me wanted to urinate in the lobby before turning around and running.

I stepped out of the elevator to the sight of Sichrovsky sitting in his office with the door open. He had close-cropped gray hair and an even tan. I sat down across from him at a small round table, removed my tape recorder and notebook from my garbage bag, and asked him why he had become a supporter of the Freedom Party.

"I've always been a political conservative," Sichrovsky said, "and in my opinion the Freedom Party was the only interesting conservative party that had the ability and the power to change the system."

Perhaps Sichrovsky could see in my expression that this answer wouldn't do. The office fell silent. I looked Sichrovsky in the eyes. He leaned back in his chair, projecting an air of confidence. "I met Mr. Haider about ten years ago in 1990," Sichrovsky continued in nearly perfect English, "and I told him, 'If you get out of your right-wing corner and become a normal conservative party, then you will make it possible for somebody like me being Jewish to work with you.' And Haider said, 'That's a good idea,' and the whole party has moved more to the center over the last ten years. Today it's a very normal conservative party, and I don't have any problems working with them."

I scribbled my notes and nodded, but I wasn't buying it. I knew enough about the Freedom Party by then to appreciate that it was not a normal conservative party. The Freedom Party's economic agenda may not differ much from that of other conservative parties, but normal conservative parties don't campaign for elections by plastering cities with posters that read STOP DER ÜBERFREMDUNG (Stop the foreign infiltration), an old Nazi propaganda slogan used by Goebbels. And the leaders of normal conservative parties don't go around praising the employment policy of the Third Reich, as Haider did in 1991. And, for that matter, rather than moving to the center, Haider had risen to power in the mid-1980s by reenergizing the more extreme elements of the Freedom Party.

I was beginning to wonder if Sichrovsky wasn't simply in denial. I asked him how he could tolerate Haider's comments about the Nazis.

"I'm not shocked by these quotes because, if you like it or not, this is the daily political style in Austria, and it has nothing to do with the Freedom Party," Sichrovsky said, growing louder and more agitated. "I can go on with a thousand comparisons and examples from the other parties, but I have to accept that the Austrian democracy was built up by ex-Nazis. I don't care about all this. For me it's more interesting to look at what the parties do—their political program, their political work. The Freedom Party has never done anything anti-Semitic. What Mr. Haider has said is a joke compared to what happened in the fifties, sixties, and seventies, when I grew up here."

Sichrovsky's voice was now just shy of a yell. "This is an atmosphere that you have to live with or you leave the country," he said. "But concerning the past of Austria, concerning the anti-Semitism, racism, and xenophobia, this is an Austrian problem and not the problem of one political party. This is a problem of Austria's postwar history, and the people of Austria have to overcome the situation and work on this problem."

Sichrovsky paused. "But the worst thing—and this has happened with the support of the Jewish organizations—is that by accusing the Freedom Party of being the bad boys here, they have freed the other two parties that were responsible, particularly the Socialists, who had the closest connection to the ex-Nazis. Now the Socialists don't see any reason to go into their own past. They feel as though they are the big antifascists, the big friends of the Jews. I'm sorry, but I have to throw up if I think about this."

Sichrovsky had come up with a clever defense: It was okay to join the Freedom Party because the other parties were also full of ex-Nazis. And he was right about the other parties, at least the other two biggest parties. The Social Democrats had made considerable progress in the last decade, but there's no escaping the party's old habit of giving former Nazis leadership positions. Even worse, the Social Democrats had helped reestablish the former Nazis as a voting bloc, in the hope that the new party would steal votes from their main competitor, the conservative People's Party. For its part, the People's Party made almost no effort over the postwar decades to purge the deep-rooted Catholic anti-Semitism that has long permeated the party. The anti-Semitism of the People's Party was never much of a secret, but it became a scandal in the wake of the Waldheim affair. Even in the face of strong evidence that Kurt Waldheim (the secretary-general of the United Nations from 1972 to 1981) had been a Nazi intelligence officer involved with the deportation of at least 70,000 Jews to Auschwitz, the People's Party supporters had elected him president of Austria in 1986 amid cries that he was a victim of a smear campaign by international Jewish organizations.

Still, Sichrovsky's reasoning was somewhat deceptive: All of the major Austrian parties might have shameful pasts, but they weren't all equally shameful. The Social-Democratic Party (then known as the Socialist Party) and the People's Party had gotten into bed with Nazis. The Freedom Party had been founded by and for Nazis. The leaders of the other parties might still be anti-Semites, but unlike the Freedom Party officials, they no longer used Nazi rhetoric in their speeches.

I should have challenged Sichrovsky, but I was overwhelmed by the forcefulness of his delivery and was also tired and not thinking clearly. I thanked him for his time and left. On my way out he handed me an autographed copy of his new book, *Jewish Love Stories.*

It was midday. I bought a black Puma bag with gold stripes on the side because a very attractive saleswoman with long blond hair and an earring in her nose had encouraged me to do so, then headed to a small shoe-repair stand, hoping that my shoes could be returned to a single color. An old man with reddish hair and a strong chin stood behind the counter, racks of shoe heels and small tools behind him. "Because you are tourist," he said, "I will polish shoes for ten schillings." I doubted that tourists received special discounts, but it sounded like a good price, and so I stood on the street in my tube socks and waited. When the old man handed my shoes back, I announced that I was a journalist and asked him what he thought of the current government.

The old man paused, then looked me up and down. "You are Jewish?"

"Yes," I said, slightly startled.

"I am Jewish," he said. "From Russia."

I smiled, but the man seemed no warmer now that we had made a connection. "And what do you think of this government and Haider?"

"More Nazis in America than here," the old man said loudly. Then he glanced at my shoes and said it again. "More Nazis in America than here."

"Do you really think so?"

The old man repeated the phrase for the third time, as though it were suddenly the only thing he knew how to say in English.

Unsure of what else to do, I paid him ten schillings for the shoeshine and walked off.

In my now even-toned shoes, I ventured into Vienna's Second District, the center of the city's large Jewish community until 1939, and made my way to Jambo, a small African restaurant where the administrators of no-racism.net had instructed me to meet them. Before I left for Austria, I had done a web search on "racism" and "Austria" and found that no-racism.net kept popping up. The site was mostly in German, and I wasn't quite sure what it was all about, but when I e-mailed and said I was a journalist, the administrators expressed interest in meeting me—no doubt assuming I was a much more important person than I am.

For five minutes I was the only white person in the restaurant. Then two men and two women from no-racism.net walked in, and they too were white. Both of the men had brought black dogs, one of which was wearing a red bandana. The younger of the two women looked about my age. She wore a tank top, and her apricot-colored hair brushed her exposed shoulders. She reminded me of the cool hippie girls I had lusted after from a distance during college.

It was too noisy to hear one another at Jambo, but before we left, one of the men—he refused to give me his real name—insisted that I interview the restaurant's owner. I walked up to the bar, where I was introduced to a tall Kenyan man named John. I asked John if he had experienced a lot of racism in Vienna, and he said that he hadn't had too many problems until six years ago, when he opened Jambo. Since then the police had repeatedly raided the restaurant, rounding up people who didn't have papers. Now and then they came looking for drugs. "Sometimes I want to close the restaurant," John said, "but I don't want them to think they've won."

I spent the next three hours talking with the no-racism.net administrators about the treatment of immigrants in Austria. They explained how Haider had manipulated anxieties about Austria's integration into the European Union to stir up anti-immigrant sentiment, and they took turns describing the cruelty of the government's response to asylum seekers.

The police brutality they described sounded a lot like what was going on in New York at the time, but one difference, I learned, was that Austrian politicians could still get away with openly racist remarks. Freedom Party officials regularly call black immigrants "drug dealers," and in past elections the party had put up signs calling on Austrians to stop Vienna from turning into Chicago—their code name for the black inner city. The year before, in a discussion of the increase in foreign doctors in Vienna, Haider had remarked, "In the future every jungle bunny [*Buschneger*] will be able to treat his kind in Austria."

"But in terms of actual treatment of the minorities and asylum seekers," I asked at one point, "has there really been a big change between this government and the last?"

There was a brief pause, then the woman in the tank top,

Irene (pronounced É-ren-e), broke the silence. "Before asylum prisoners had to do a hunger strike for two weeks to get the government to respond," she said. "Now you have to do it for three weeks."

I liked the response and the giggle that followed it. When we parted, I thought about asking her out, but I was supposed to be a professional journalist, and besides, I'd never had the confidence to ask out a woman I didn't know, let alone when my nose hair might be visible.

On the U-bahn ride home, I sat across from a tall African man. I felt like an idiot. All this time I had been thinking only about Jews, but the Freedom Party, I was coming to understand, was a greater threat to the new immigrants from Africa and Eastern Europe. The best way to memorialize Austria's Jews, I thought, was to fight for the Nigerians and Bulgarians and Slovenes and Slovaks. They were the Austrian Jews of today.

# Sixteen

# How Funny to
# See You Again

Hans wasn't scheduled to return home until the next evening, and in the morning Christine and I had plans to go to the Kunsthistorisches Museum together to see the El Greco exhibit.

On the way to the museum Christine told me that prior to Hans, the love of her life had been a man named Peter, who had committed suicide. "He was very extreme," Christine said, "maybe more extreme than Hans." She said Peter was also Jewish, also something of a philosopher, and, amazingly, had also worked with sheep, although only briefly and not as a shepherd.

"How did you manage to find two Jewish men in Austria who had worked with sheep?" I asked.

"I was looking for people who understand," Christine said, "people who know what is psychological pain even if it is a different psychological pain from mine."

"Well, if you were looking for psychological pain, Hans was a great choice," I said.

"Yes," Christine said without smiling.

~

In the museum, surrounded by El Greco's anxiously gesturing Christians, I saw Irene standing next to an older woman.

I thought about approaching her, but what would I possibly say? I could start with *Hey there*, but then she'd say, *Hi* or *Hey*, and then what would I say? *What's going on? What's up?* It was impossible.

I looked at El Greco's sensuous Mary Magdalene gazing heavenward, her lilac cloak falling off her creamy shoulders. Then I turned to the corner of the room, put my index finger under my nose to check for the hair, and walked over to Irene.

"Hey," I said.

"Hi," she said. "How funny to see you again." She was wearing another tank top. Her hair was pulled back, but she had left out one sexy wisp to dangle over the right side of her face. She had brown eyes and piercings up and down her ears.

"Yeah, it's really funny," I said.

"I'm here with my mom," Irene said.

"Cool," I said. "So is there anything to do in Vienna at night?" Irene said that yes, in fact, there are things to do in

Vienna at night and that if I'd like, she could show me one of them. We made plans to meet at a bar on the Danube called Flex later that evening.

I had a date with a woman I barely knew. It called for a celebration. I briefly entertained the idea of running up to the museum guard and giving him a leaping chest thump, then thought better of it and quietly returned to Mary Magdalene. It felt a little bit like a miracle.

⌐⁓⁓

Hans arrived at Christine's apartment tired and dirty later that afternoon.

"How were the last few days?" I asked.

Hans shook his head. "With Kati, there is always difficulties," he said, pulling off his shirt. I could see the exhaustion in his eyes and in the slight droop of his jaw.

Unlike me, Hans has no issues about stripping in front of others, and the next thing I knew, he was naked in Christine's hallway shower singing a Yiddish love song about a mother who goes to the market to buy coal and returns with a groom with "little black eyes" for her daughter. After the shower Hans put on what I assumed was Christine's silk Chinese robe and announced that he was going to be on TV in a few minutes—an Austrian film crew had spent a few days taping him for a popular nature program. Christine joined us in front of the TV in the spare bedroom.

The segment lasted five minutes and showed Hans, Kati, Andi, and Wolfi walking in the mountains. There was footage of Hans calling to the sheep and of Kati yanking a goo-covered lamb from its mother's womb with alarming force.

I was about to congratulate Hans when it ended, but he didn't look at all pleased. "You see they create this fairy tale for television," he said, turning off the TV.

Christine nodded. "They want to show Hans and Kati like it is one happy family," she said. "They don't like to show the reality."

"You will tell the real story," Hans said with a glum smile.

Later it occurred to me that the TV program had made no mention of Hans's Yiddish singing.

I asked Hans about this omission, and he said the director wasn't interested in his singing. "I told him about it, but he wanted only to tell the story of shepherd in the countryside," Hans said. "This would be what the TV audience here would like to see."

Irene was sitting in the dark at an outdoor picnic table in front of Flex. The bar was on the bank of the Danube, and it was chilly. She wore an orange zip-up sweatshirt, the hood resting between her shoulder blades.

"Hey," I said.

"Hey," she said.

We bought beers and talked casually for a minute, then Irene took out a lighter that was covered in what looked like rubbery Hershey's Kisses.

"I make these," she said, noticing my interest. "I sell them from my bike at all the antigovernment rallies."

"That's awesome," I said.

"Do you smoke marijuana?" she asked.

I thought back to the last time I had tried years earlier: After two hits I had declared to a roomful of people that I was having an asthma attack and had to be talked out of calling 911.

"Sure," I said.

Irene handed me the silicon-covered lighter and a tightly rolled joint.

"You first."

I put the joint between my lips and flicked at the lighter's wheel with my thumb. Nothing. I flicked again. Then again. Nothing. *This woman will never have sex with me,* I thought.

Irene took the lighter from me without asking. I felt her skin on mine.

"You don't smoke much?" she said.

I shrugged, and she lit the joint, still perched between my lips. I did my best to inhale.

Next to us a group of teenagers, also sharing a joint, occasionally broke into song. Later one of them came over to Irene and said something about the Führer. When she handed them her lighter, I understood that he had said *Feuer,* or "fire."

The smell of pot was thick in the air. The Danube moved quietly behind us. I asked Irene a lot of questions about herself and she said, "Pfu," as in, *That's a tough one,* again and again before answering. She told me that when she wasn't protesting or working on the no-racism website, she was writing her thesis on refugee children living in Vienna and doing freelance Web design.

I told her about Hans and the sheep and the shit and the *hop hops.* Probably the drugs kicked in right around then, because Irene began to laugh fairly hard. Then I too began to giggle for long stretches, hoping that we weren't really laughing at what an idiot I was.

When the conversation turned serious, Irene told me that her father died a year before and that she still missed him every day.

She was a hippie with a serious side, a free spirit who had more or less devoted her life to fighting for the rights of minorities in Austria. Nothing could have impressed me more at that moment. I was smitten, and maybe a little drunk.

Irene lived near Christine, and we agreed to take the train back together. When I stopped to buy a ticket, Irene laughed at me. The Viennese subways don't require tickets to get on the train and instead rely upon occasional raids, or "controls," as Irene called them, during which the police stop the train and check everyone's ticket. I hadn't yet experienced one of these raids, but the entire system struck me as an incredibly bad idea. Even if you've purchased a ticket, it's not particularly relaxing to know that at any minute your train might be raided by German-speaking cops.

"But what will we do if there's a control?" I asked.

"We'll run as fast as we can," she said, walking ahead of me and laughing.

On the one hand, I could hardly think of a worse scenario for my Nazi-ridden psyche than to have Austrian police chasing me through the streets of Vienna. On the other hand, a small and rather stupid part of me liked the thought that I was cheating the anti-Semitic bastards out of fifty cents.

Just moments before my stop, I turned to Irene. "Will we stay in touch?" I asked.

"Why not?" she said. We were at my station.

"But I don't have your number," I said, stepping off the train.

"Okay," Irene said, laughing, "I'll give it to you." She jumped out of the train seconds before the doors closed. It was just before midnight, and we were the only two people on the Johnstrasse platform. We looked at each other.

"This doesn't make any sense," Irene said.

I wasn't sure what she meant, but I liked the reference to the "this." Until that moment I hadn't been sure there was a "this."

I leaned forward and she leaned forward and we pecked on the lips.

"Does this make any sense?" she asked, looking up at me.

*Hell no*, I thought. *You're Catholic and Austrian, and I'm obsessed with what your people did to my people, and besides, this can't make sense because things like this don't happen to me—I can barely make eye contact with women, let alone get them to kiss me in subway stations.*

"I don't know," I said.

Irene put her hands on my chest and ran them down my stomach, and we walked back to my apartment together.

In bed, Irene's body pressed against mine, I made a crack about my being a Jew and her being an Austrian. Irene told me she didn't like to look at things that way.

"I'm just joking around," I said.

"It's not funny," she said. "We're both just people."

## Seventeen

# Escape from Vienna

Hans was in the back room on the night in 1972 when the neo-Nazis threw a Molotov cocktail through the window of the Spartakus apartment. He heard the smash of the glass and the squeal of car tires, but by the time he ran outside, the assailants were gone.

That night the Spartakus members gathered around the table and debated their next step. The bomb, in their eyes, was more evidence of what they had been saying all along: The fascists were again preparing to destroy their political enemies. The street thugs weren't the only threat. The Austrian authorities were also cracking down. One member of the group had been charged with kidnapping a reformatory escapee he had helped to hide from the police. Another member had received a death threat from an officer in the

Austrian army. The stakes had risen. Something had to be done.

The meeting, like all Spartakus meetings, was led by the leader of the group, a dark-haired Frenchman named Roland Perrot. Going by the nickname Remi, Perrot arrived in Vienna in 1968, claiming to be on the run from the French police for his involvement in the May '68 student revolt in Paris. After Remi died in 1993, one of his supposed fellow combatants in the "international brigade" revealed that rather than fighting in the streets, Remi had been in a psychiatric institution prior to his arrival in Vienna. But there was no way for Hans or the others to know this at the time. They saw Remi, then in his midthirties, as the only adult who understood their anger, and they were mesmerized by his stories of fighting in the student barricades.

As the members of Spartakus sat around the table in silence, Remi told them that it was time to abandon Austria. Spartakus was being intentionally provoked, and the group's best strategy was to avoid the trap being set for them. Away from Austria they could regroup and create their own settlement, a place that would be entirely free of capitalist corruption and bankrupt bourgeois values.

Before the project had been merely to create a new type of human being. Now they would create an entirely new society. There would be no egos, no jealously, no private property, and no wages. And, most important of all, no one would put his own interests above the group's. "Our plan was to create a Cuba in Europe," Hans said with a laugh.

Not everyone in the group agreed that fleeing the country was the best strategy. In a brief account of his years with Spartakus, Michael Genner, the accused kidnapper, de-

scribes the decision to leave Austria as a disastrous misjudg-
ment. "We could have joined in the left movement that had
arisen in Austria—arisen not least through us," Genner
writes. "But—we fled. We ourselves gave up. . . . It was the
decisive mistake from which all the other mistakes derived."

Hans, near the bottom of the Spartakus hierarchy, had
no say in the matter. Remi was the undisputed leader, and
he had made up his mind.

## Eighteen

# Love in the Time
# of Anti-Semitism

In one eighteenth-century version of the legend, the Wandering Jew isn't the only one giving Jesus a hard time. The Wandering Jew's wife also has a few unkind words for Jesus when she finds him loitering on the family doorstep, and, as is only fair, she too is ordered to wander for eternity. To ensure that the punishment's isolationist ethos isn't undermined, the Wandering Jew and Jewess are forced to wander in opposite directions. It's a nice tragic touch, and the author might have left it there, husband and wife doomed to parallel lives of longing. But in a wonderful romantic twist, we learn that the two are allowed to meet for a single hour once every hundred years. You might think these meetings would be a good time for the Jew and the Jewess, a chance perhaps to make love and then to quickly catch up on the last century.

Instead, their joy at seeing each other is instantly overwhelmed by the devastating thought that it will be another hundred years before they experience the same joy again.

When I think of this story, I sometimes think of the pain that would overtake Hans's face at the very sight of Kati. Other times I think of my own problems with women.

The next morning after Irene left, a bout of depression hit me out of nowhere. I had all the symptoms: the pit in the stomach, the heavy eyes, the recurring thought that life is little more than endless suffering, interspersed, if you're lucky, with a good meal or two.

I sat at the foot of the bed and tried to force myself to think about the championship years of the Houston Rockets, my favorite basketball team. I've been turning to the Rockets to block out bad thoughts since I was five or six. My father had suggested the technique back then, hoping that it would stop me from coming to his room every night out of a fear that there was a *ganef* (thief) hanging out in the small space between my bunk beds and the wall.

The technique has been generally successful (and I strongly recommend it to others), but that morning not even the Rockets could help me. No sooner would I call up an image of Hakeem Olajuwon shaking off a double-team than the seven-foot-tall Nigerian would turn into a five-foot-six Austrian giggling at me through a haze of smoke. Irene had left only minutes ago, and yet I felt a powerful urge to see her again, almost as though I needed proof that she would still be there.

I'm not sure what sparked my depression that morning. My best guess is that, knowing I would be leaving Austria soon, my brain had decided to get a head start on the sense of loss I would experience when I separated from Irene. I am not good at many things, but I might be least good of all at saying good-bye to a woman I'm involved with. I met my first girlfriend in Israel when I was a sophomore in high school. She was also an American, and when we returned to the United States—she to Maryland, I to Texas—we maintained a long-distance relationship for a year. We visited each other several times, and when we would part at the airport, I would feel as though I literally were not going to make it, as though I were going to fold over and crumple to the floor and perhaps get run over by a beeping cart with old people perched precariously on the back.

My mini-breakdown that morning continued throughout my train ride to Carinthia, where I was going to interview Adi Wimmer, a professor of English at the University of Klagenfurt. Klagenfurt is the capital of Carinthia, the southernmost Austrian province, known for its Mediterranean climate, its beautiful mountains and lakes, and its people's dislike of their Slovenian neighbors. Because Carinthia is Haider's power base, it was a natural place for me to explore the anti-immigrant prejudices that had contributed to the Freedom Party's recent electoral success. But I had stupidly scheduled an interview in Vienna the following morning and would have no time to hang out in Klagenfurt.

I met Wimmer at a campus pizza shop. Before my trip I had come across a book of interviews with Austrian Jewish exiles Wimmer had edited called *Strangers at Home and Abroad*, and I had been captivated by Wimmer's personal story in the introduction as much as by the heart-wrenching accounts of the Austrian exiles.

Wimmer was born in Braunau am Inn, Austria, in

1949. He had a thin red beard and spoke with the fluidity of a university lecturer. Although he now goes by Adi, just four years after the war his parents named him Adolf after his father. This name might have been a burden anywhere, but in Braunau, the city in Upper Austria where Hitler was born, it carried extra weight. "There were men who would laugh and give me the Hitler salute, and say, 'Oh, you are our new Führer,' " Wimmer told me. "I would stand by speechless, not knowing what was going on."

Wimmer first learned about the Holocaust from reading journals, which, in those days, his family would rent for a week. In one of those journals he saw pictures of the concentration camps for the first time. "Imagine an impressionable seven-year-old seeing these mountains of dead, the heaps, the bodies, and the bulldozers, and all of that," Wimmer said. "I turned to my mother, and she said, 'This is Adolf Hitler's doing.' So I saw the mountains of the dead, and I understood that it had something to do with somebody called Adolf, my own name. That probably never left me. I was saddled with this name that stood for something really evil."

Echoing stories Hans had told me, Wimmer described the Austria of his childhood as a place where you didn't talk about National Socialism or Jews. "There is one enduring memory about asking questions on the war," Wimmer writes in the introduction to his book. "I would always be told that there was no point in talking about it 'yet again.' " On one of the few occasions when the subject did come up in school, Wimmer remembers his history teacher making "glassy-eyed speculations about the glorious future Braunau would have had 'if we had only won the war.' "

Wimmer also remembers how tourists would come to see

the house where Hitler was born. Embarrassed to publicly reveal their destination, the Führer enthusiasts would ask local children to help them find the residence. When he was thirteen, Wimmer led one man to the house, then "watched in fascination" as the man chipped mortar from the wall to take home as a souvenir.

As I stuffed my face with an overly cheesy pizza, Wimmer told me about the Austrian exiles he had interviewed. The stories were heartbreaking. Edward Arie, one of the Austrian exiles Wimmer spoke with, was arrested and tortured by the SS, then sent to Dachau, where he barely survived his seven-week stay. Although Arie managed to flee, his father was killed. In the early 1990s it looked as though Austria was finally going to make reparation payments to Arie, but after he worked on his application for seven months, he was told that since he was over eighteen at the time of his father's death, he could not be compensated for the loss. For his seven weeks at Dachau, Arie was offered $150. Arie returned the check with a polite note. He died a year later. "The thought that this kind, unblemished man went to the grave without receiving justice from my country has haunted me ever since," Wimmer writes in his book.

Another thing that troubles Wimmer is his country's failure to invite Austrian exiles to visit their native country. Unlike the German Jewish exiles, who have been offered free trips back to Germany and who are often treated as honored guests, the vast majority of Austrian Jews who fled for their lives during the Nazi years have been ignored by postwar Austrian governments. In one instance, Wimmer wrote a letter to the Austrian city of Baden suggesting they invite two ex-Badeners living abroad to visit the city where they were born. In a written response from the mayor, Wimmer was told to mind his own business.

On the ride back to Vienna, I had a six-seat compartment to myself. After listening to Wimmer's stories, I was feeling a little less depressed and a lot more angry. And while I preferred the anger to the depression, it felt equally useless.

It's not that there are no outlets for rage against the Nazis. I could probably do a million small things to make the world a better place, to ensure that hateful ideologies never again make their way into the mainstream. But as the train cut through the Styrian countryside, I had another idea. I could masturbate. I had arrived in Vienna to find a semenlike substance on my backpack. Now I would return the gesture by leaving a semenlike substance on an Austrian train.

You jerk off on me, I jerk off on you.

In the short-story version of my trip, this would be the denouement, the moment when all the different emotions that had been rumbling inside of me would come together in one triumphantly irrational act. I would whip it out and stick it in the window for the entire Nazi country to see. Old and young anti-Semites alike would gaze in confusion as my circumcised penis sped by. Readers would understand that even as I was lashing out against Austria, I was lashing out against myself, against all the neuroses and sexual hang-ups that had left me, in my midtwenties, still trying to smooth over the troubled relationship between my Jewish identity and my johnson. Alex Portnoy goes to the camps!

But I wasn't a character. My pants stayed on. Still, the

thought that my penis might be a tool of vengeance was now in the air, and soon it began to morph into even more disturbing thoughts. What if there was something dark in my desire for Irene? What if I was unconsciously conflating lust and anger? The last thing I wanted was for an innocent woman to become a pawn in my psychosexual antics.

I put my head down on an empty seat next to me and thought about the Rockets.

When I made it back to Vienna that evening, Hans and Christine and Wolfi were relaxing around the kitchen table. Hans suggested we play a board game called Action Professional, a version of charades in which players are required to act out German proverbs. Regardless of the proverb he was trying to convey, Hans would get out of his chair and flail around the kitchen. I probably hadn't laughed so hard since I had first seen Hans in concert singing in front of his slides of sheep, and the comic relief couldn't have come at a better time.

Christine tried to explain the proverbs to me, but it was no use, and I was content to watch Hans and laugh and wonder what in the hell he was trying to get me to understand. Another good metaphor, I thought, this one for my entire project.

After the game Hans came back to my apartment with me to help me iron my suit (I accepted his offer to help because even though I know how to iron, things don't look right when I do them) and told me about the tremendous guilt he had experienced throughout his relationship with Kati.

I don't remember how the conversation started, but I remember Hans leaning over my dress pants, iron in hand, telling me that his eldest son, Günter, had recently been helping him to see that he was "not such bad person."

Something about the son convincing the father of his worth made me sad.

"What did Günter say?" I asked.

"He tells me all these things with Kati are not only my fault," Hans said. "My problem was that I was always a little bit trapped in this role of chasing Kati. For years I was thinking that if only I am not bad person and not always wanting too much attention and sex, perhaps we would have better relationship." Hans sprayed boiling water from the head of the iron onto my pants. "I did cause many problems with my wrong behaviors, but in the last years I was working very hard to change my comportment."

As I stood next to Hans, watching him iron, he fell into one of his spells of raw honesty. "I was on my knees for Kati," he told me. "It was horrible. I would try to tell myself there are other women in the world, but I was not feeling there are other women in the world. For months I did not sleep, but would go out every night, coming back at three in the morning. I was suffering. My friends would say, 'Oh, you must not go on like this,' but they could not help me because I did not want to be helped."

I asked Hans if he knew that the dentist was a threat before he left for America.

"Yes, he is my dentist," Hans said. "I have known him many years."

His own dentist! I had no idea. "Well, I guess you've found a new person to clean your teeth," I said.

Hans looked up from his ironing. "No, he is still my dentist," he said.

"Come on!"

"He is good dentist, and I am not so weak that I must run away because of these things."

I wasn't sure what to say. Hans told me that during this period of grief, he had gone through a very rare three-month stretch without sex.

"I missed this movement," he said, putting down the iron and thrusting his hips gently. He wasn't joking. "If you have sex alone," Hans continued, "you don't move this area." He pointed to his crotch. "How do you say it?"

"Pelvis?"

"Yes, pelvis. When you are alone, you move only your hand, and I was starting to miss this movement." Hans thrusted again. "This was new for me. After some time I was looking for woman on every corner."

"You should have gone on the Internet," I said, joking.

"Yes, I thought maybe I would do this," Hans said.

**HANS BREUER'S ONLINE DATING PROFILE**

**User name:** SheepGuy2001

**Age:** 46

**Occupation:** Wandering shepherd

**Interests:** Yiddish folksinging, intercourse

**In my bedroom you'll find:** My three sons and a big hat

**For a good time I like to:** Talk about the lack of denazification in Austria

Hans put down my pants and picked up my jacket. I told him about Irene. "It's strange," I said. "I barely know her, but already there's this powerful feeling of vulnerability."

"Yes, I know very well this feeling," Hans said. "But does she understand you well?"

"I think so," I said.

"Good," Hans said. "This is important."

"The worst part of the feeling," I said, "is that it makes you insecure, and then the woman is less attracted to you. I think this was part of your problem with Kati. Sometimes the best strategy is to pretend to be confident."

"There was no strategy with Kati," Hans said, "only what was inside of myself."

Hans's honesty sometimes made me feel like an asshole. I watched him in silence for a moment. Then I told him that journalists didn't usually have their subjects iron their suits. Hans didn't see the humor. "It is okay," he said. "Now when I say good night to you with the Yiddish words *shlof gezunt, shtey uf gezunt,* I feel a little bit like you are a son to me."

It was outrageous. I had really only known the guy for a few weeks. But that was Hans, and I knew he meant it. I gave him an awkward pat on the arm.

# Nineteen

# In the Army

**H**ans turned the doorknob over and over. He was trapped. The officer had locked him in a supply shed of the Austrian army without food or a bathroom. Hans pounded on the door and kicked it a few times with his army boots. Then he slumped to the floor in frustration, all too aware of the irony of the situation. He had decided by age twelve that he would never go into the army, even if he was sent to jail for twenty years. Now he was in the Austrian army and imprisoned in a storage shed while his friends were busy creating a new society.

At the time military service was required of all Austrian men (now they can choose to do communal service instead), but Hans could have avoided the army by fleeing Austria with the others. He enlisted on Remi's orders. Remi thought it would be good to have Hans "on the inside," learning the enemy's techniques so that he would make a good partisan when the fighting broke out. Hans went along with the idea because, deep down, he wanted nothing more than to be a good partisan.

Hans got into trouble almost immediately upon enlisting. He was repeatedly punished and sometimes briefly imprisoned for not showing sufficient respect to his officers. "They shout at you and insult you from early to late in the evening," Hans recalled. "But I showed them I would not be their slave. And somebody who is not a slave in the heart will never be a slave."

Several months into Hans's tour of duty, after he and his unit had failed to return from a training exercise that required them to hide in the forest, the Austrian army came to its senses and moved Hans to a desk job in a supply room. Even there Hans managed to be a nuisance, and so an officer had locked him in the supply shed for the entire day. That night, when the officer came to let Hans out, Hans had a surprise for him. "I gave him my shit in box," Hans told me.

After six months Hans left the army, anxious to rejoin Remi and the others. Over the next two and a half years, he would discover that Spartakus had, in fact, created a new society—just not the one he had anticipated.

Twenty

# Kiss Me, I'm Jewish

The next morning I put on my crisply ironed suit and found an old yarmulke in the pocket. I stuffed it into my bag and headed downtown, where I spoke with a member of Vienna's organized Jewish community. Hans, Christine, and Hans's son Günter met me downtown. Günter was thin but well built. His long brown bangs gave him the air of a member of the Partridge Family. Either because he was shy or didn't like me or had no idea who I was and why I was taking notes on his father's every utterance, he kept his distance after we were introduced.

We spent the afternoon touring some of Vienna's World War II memorials. At Albertinaplatz, where several hundred people were killed in a 1945 air raid, we looked at the Memorial Against War and Fascism. Erected by Alfred

Hrdlicka from 1981 to 1991—over protests from conservative politicians—the abstract carving of twisted bodies was a
dramatic departure from the typical Austrian war memorial
dedicated to the "heroes" who "defended the fatherland."
Vienna had not been ready for a memorial devoted only to
Jews, but Hrdlicka's piece does include a small sculpture of
a bearded Jew scrubbing the street. The Jew is crouched on
his hands and knees, and there is barbed wire on his back—
the barbed wire hadn't been a part of the original memorial
but was added when it was discovered that the Viennese
were using the street-scrubbing Jew as a bench.

Vienna finally got a memorial dedicated specifically to
Austria's Jewish victims in 2000. The work of British sculp-
tor Rachel Whiteread, the monument is a twelve-foot-high
white square meant to resemble a library with the books
turned backward so that their spines can't be viewed. At the
base of the monument are the names of the camps where
65,000 Austrian Jews were killed.

The Jewish memorial occupies a good portion of Judenplatz, a baroque square where archaeologists have uncovered
the remains of a fifteenth-century synagogue destroyed when
several hundred Jews burned themselves alive inside rather
than submit to baptism. You can still see a sixteenth-century
relief in the square with a Latin inscription commemorating
the death of the "Hebrew dogs." The Catholic Church recently added a plaque that apologizes for the Church's his-
toric role in stirring up hatred against Jews and refers to the
fifteenth-century attacks as "an ominous portent for what
happened, in our century, all over Europe during the National Socialist dictatorship."

From Judenplatz, the others went back to Christine's

apartment, but it was Thursday, and I wanted to check out a new Viennese tradition. Every Thursday night since the new government had formed in February of 2000, there had been a rally and march through downtown Vienna. The protestors met in Ballhausplatz, a small square from which you can gaze on the sprawling Hofburg (Imperial Palace) to the east and on the parliament building to the west. In the first months the marches had drawn thousands. On that Thursday in June, more than a year later, there were only a hundred or so protesters, a motley mix of potbellied ex-hippies and young leftists in Che Guevara T-shirts. It wasn't exactly May '68, but considering that the marches had been going on every week for a year, it was an impressive turnout. And there was discontent in the air. On the sidewalk someone had chalked *FPÖ: Fascho Partei Österreich*. Banners and flags bearing the word *Widerstand* (resistance) fluttered in the light breeze. Under a small tent, set up by the organizers, you could buy I DIDN'T VOTE FOR THIS GOVERNMENT postcards and GIVE NAZIS NO CHANCE shirts.

I looked around for Irene, but she wasn't there. It had been less than forty-eight hours since I had seen her, but already our night together was beginning to feel like a dream. I wanted to call her, but I was scared, convinced she had awakened in the morning thinking that the whole thing hadn't made any sense after all.

Around me the protesters gathered in groups and chatted. I asked a young woman dressed in all black why she had come to the march. "The FPÖ is using harmful language," she said. "Also, there's so much stupid racism and sexism in this government." She stopped to think for a moment, then continued. "We are showing the world that not all Austrians are Nazis."

Off to the side, several dozen policemen waited to escort the marchers through the city. Three of the policemen near me stood shoulder to shoulder, looking straight ahead. Unsure of which of the three to address, I announced to all of them that I was a journalist from New York. They seemed unimpressed. The line had failed me for the first time. "I'm here from New York to write about Austria," I said again. The meanest looking of the three told me I could ask him questions if I didn't use my tape recorder.

I brought up the charges I had heard about racism in the Austrian police force. The officer said there was no such thing as racism in the Austrian police force. As I stood fumbling for another question, the march started and I began to walk along with the officers. When I looked up from my notebook, I found myself in the middle of a circle of about ten Austrian policemen.

I escaped and joined the protesters, who were now banging drums and blowing whistles. Walking through the heart of the city, I took in Vienna's grand buildings and creamy palaces and thought about how awful it would be to have to paint them. An old woman with long white hair and a red whistle around her neck was shouting at a few of the other marchers. I was sure I heard her use the word "anti-Semite," and concerned that I might have just missed an interesting exchange, I asked her what was going on.

"I'm telling them they shouldn't bring their dogs with them," the old woman said, and then she looked into my eyes inquisitively, as though she recognized me.

"You must be Armenian," she said.

"No," I said, smiling. "But I'll take that as a compliment."

"Yes, it's a compliment," she said. She looked at me again, her face now scrunched in confusion.

"But you must be Armenian," she said.

Again I denied it. We went back and forth several more times on this point until she gave up and asked me where my family was from.

"Originally from Poland and Lithuania," I said.

The old woman looked suspicious.

"I'm Jewish," I said.

With that, she grabbed my neck, pulled me strongly toward her, and kissed me hard on the cheek. When I broke free, she gazed at me, eyes full of disbelief. "What are you doing in this country?" she asked.

"Just hanging out," I said.

The woman, who I was beginning to think was drunk, smiled, blew her whistle a few times, and walked on.

I walked on as well, still shaken from the embrace. I had been kissed for being a Jew. In this case it was clearly some sort of creepy philo-Semitism, but it left me wondering if Irene too had kissed me for being a Jew. Maybe, despite her insistence that she didn't want to think of things that way, she couldn't help seeing our affair—or whatever it was—through the lens of the Holocaust any more than I could. Maybe, at some only partially conscious level, she had gone to bed with me to make amends for what her countrymen had done to the Jews.

I suppose this insight should have troubled me, especially

since I felt terrible about the possibility that I had become involved with her for the wrong reasons. And yet, try as I did to feel used, I couldn't quite muster it. *By all means,* I thought, *ķiss me for being a Jew. Give me a blow job for being a Jew. Let all the young attractive women in the country worķ through their guilt in bed with me. Hell, the German women might as well get in on the act too.*

The thought that Irene might like me for the wrong reasons gave me an unexpected boost of confidence. It was the first time since I had awoken next to her that I considered that she might like me at all.

I broke away from the march and found a pay phone to call her.

"I want to see you again," I said.

"Yes, that would be fun," she said.

I met Irene for a picnic the next day, in the shadow of the Neue Burg (New Wing) of the Hofburg Palace. The building that had once been the seat of one of the world's great empires was now occupied by an assortment of museums and government offices. We spread out a blanket on the same lawn that sixty years earlier had been filled with tens of thousands of delirious Austrians cheering on Hitler as he addressed them from the balcony of the Hofburg upon his arrival in Vienna in 1938. I had brought a yogurt drink and chocolate eggs that come with toys inside. Irene had brought cherries, a bag of mini-croissants, chocolate spread, and a thick joint she had rolled for the occasion. As I nibbled on my egg, Irene told me about her childhood. She had grown up in a Catholic family. On special occasions the family dressed in traditional Austrian attire.

"You wear a dirndl?" I asked.

Irene giggled. "Why not?"

It seemed a bit ridiculous, although I suppose she would find it equally ridiculous were she to picture me in synagogue with a white shawl around my shoulders and a round piece of cloth on my head.

I asked Irene if she had witnessed a lot of anti-Semitism in Austria. "Yes, but of course," she said. "Little kids on the playground would tell lots of Jewish jokes. And in school I went on a trip to Mauthausen with my class, and it was scary. Most of the students were more interested in where to get the best desserts than in the concentration camp."

*Those fuckers*, I thought.

"Kids will be kids," I said.

"No, they were sixteen," she said. "They don't realize how recently it happened, that people who did these things are still alive."

Irene also told me that Austrians, even those who don't intend to be anti-Semitic, regularly use the expression *bis zur Vergasung* ("to the point of gassing [someone]") to mean "ad nauseam."

Ten yards from us, a man and a woman were sitting cross-legged and juggling oranges. I tried to put together the minitrain that had come in my egg. Irene smoked her joint. I took a few entirely ineffective hits and then lay down on my back and looked at the neo-Renaissance pillars of the Hofburg in silence.

"What should we do next?" Irene said.

"Well, we could always go make love in the Hofburg," I said, entirely joking, although fully prepared to act on the joke should Irene give a remotely positive response.

"Good idea," she said, and so we walked into the Hofburg. And so, to my own amazement, I found myself with my pants around my ankles, crouching under a stairway of the Hapsburgs' famous residence—in the very wing of the building where Hitler had triumphantly declared Austria a part of the German Reich. And so, to my horror, moments later an elderly janitor discovered me with my pants around my ankles crouching beneath the stairway of the Hapsburgs' famous residence in the very wing of the building where Hitler had triumphantly declared Austria a part of the German Reich.

In a flash I saw a photo of myself pantless and in handcuffs on the front page of the local papers: JEWISH TOURIST CAUGHT FONDLING LOCAL WOMAN IN HOFBURG.

But the janitor smirked and walked on. I pulled up my pants and we hurried out.

# Twenty-one

# "The Terrible Breuer"

Remi had decided to move Spartakus to France, but first the group stopped in Switzerland, where they merged with a revolutionary Swiss outfit known as Hydra and set about gathering funds for the new commune. To collect donations, the young radicals would sometimes ride through the streets of Basel in a horse-drawn wagon, eliciting the sympathies of the very petit bourgeois liberals they despised for not joining their revolution. The Swiss members brought in most of the money. Several of them came from wealthy families, and one had ties to a large chemical company that agreed to support the new settlement. In Hans's memory, the irony that the new society would be funded by the same corrupt system the group hoped to one day overthrow didn't cause much internal strife among the members.

On June 14, 1973, the Spartakus/Hydra collective bought 300 hectares in Provence for the price of 521,500 francs. The new settlement was dubbed Longo Maï ("May It Last Long" in Provençal), and the original two-dozen "pioneers," as they called themselves, immediately got to work. Spotted with fields of lavender and thyme, the rocky, arid landscape wasn't well suited to farming (the locals had already mostly given up), but the barren earth turned out to be no match for the group's idealism. They fixed up the dilapidated barn that came with the property, dug a reservoir, installed a pipe system for irrigation, and laid out vegetable gardens. At night, when the work was done, they slept outside or all together on the straw-covered floor of the barn. With money flowing in from Switzerland, they were able to buy expensive tools and farm animals. An old Longo Maï document I found among Hans's papers lists the following initial purchases: "3 tractors (large, medium, small); agricultural machinery; axes, machetes, sickles, shovel . . . 120 sheep."

After his six months in the army, Hans made his way to Longo Maï, only to be stunned by what he found. Remi, now referred to as "the Great Educator," had transformed himself from the leader of a youthful political outfit into the guru of a utopian cult. Remi had always been an authoritarian figure, but during the Spartakus years it was still possible to question him. At Longo Maï his authority was absolute. Remi dictated not just what vegetables the collective should grow, but also who should perform which jobs and often even who should sleep with whom. One of the worst offenses within Longo Maï in the mid-1970s was to carry on a monogamous relationship, and Remi spent a good portion of his time fighting what became known as "the war against the couples."

In a book about representations of Longo Maï in the media, the French journalist Gilbert Caty tells the story of a woman named Dominique who felt "criminalized" for refusing to follow Remi's orders to sleep around. "I wanted a child, yet I also wanted to be sure that my boyfriend was the father," Dominique says.

Michael Genner, who had been one of the intellectual leaders of the group, was outraged by Remi's constant abuse of couples. "What [Remi] was able to do in Longo Maï was to totally pervert our old objective: sexual freedom," Genner writes in his reflections. "In place of free love stood the subjugation of people to the collective."

Most of the hundreds of young people who came to live at Longo Maï in the '70s soon left of their own accord. Others who wouldn't submit to Remi's demands were chased away. If a new arrival was young and male and particularly compliant, he might be invited into what became known as Remi's "Boys' Group." Made up of a handful of young men between the ages of fifteen and twenty, the group lived separately with Remi in a hut atop the hill and held a special status in the community.

Hans had been driven to Spartakus, at least in part, by a sense of inadequacy in the face of his mother's suffering and heroics. But Spartakus had only added a new sense of inadequacy. Remi would mock and even beat members of the group outside of his small circle of power. Because he was one of the youngest members of Spartakus, and because he remained a strong individualist, Hans had always been a favorite target for Remi's abuses. When he wasn't ridiculing Hans for sport, Remi would tell him that his ego was too strong and that everything he did was doomed to failure be-cause he wanted success and praise too badly.

"The picture he drew of me was exaggerated, but I think Remi was maybe right in how he saw me," Hans said. "But he left me with no way to deal with my problems other than to play the fool. He fixed me in that role of 'the terrible Breuer.' I always felt there was something wrong with me be-cause I was the only one who could not live up to Remi's ideas of how human beings should be."

Looking back, Hans feels a different sort of guilt—guilt for being a part of Remi's system, for standing by as others were slapped and humiliated in the name of the collective. "My conscience, my common sense, I had mostly switched off," Hans said. "I didn't see the injustice that happened be-fore my eyes in this group every day and even less the shit I myself did. And yet I could not leave. It was clear to me—if I leave this group, where the new human is created, then it's like I'm going to hell. Then it's like I'm dead, I'm nothing." Hans paused. "It was like you leave your mother forever."

# Twenty-two

# Meet the Parents

I saw Hans perform in Austria for the first time later that week. The concert was in the basement of Christine's building, where she was holding an opening in the small gallery she had set up in two bare, white rooms.

When I walked in, Hans was already singing "Tum Balalaika," a Yiddish classic that I remembered from a fifth-grade music class at my Jewish day school. It's a song about a young man's search for the perfect bride. In despair, the young man asks a riddle: "Maiden, Maiden," he says, "I want to ask you something: What can grow without rain? What can burn without being consumed? What can cry without tears?" "Silly boy," the maiden responds, "why do you need to ask? A stone can grow without rain. Love can burn without being consumed. The heart can cry without tears." As Hans's voice rose higher and higher with the ascending melody, the audience members, some of them holding glasses of red wine, tapped their feet.

I wasn't sure how to feel about the scene. All along, Hans's concerts had struck me as something just shy of a heroic act. I imagined the Austrian audience members covered in sweat like the protagonist of *A Clockwork Orange* absorbing the painful truth with his eyelids taped open. But watching these Viennese yuppies bopping to the music, it hardly seemed like Hans was reeducating anyone. No, this wasn't how it was supposed to be. These people were enjoying Hans's concert way too much.

The short-story moment came to me in a flash: *I stand up, walk into the center of the room, and begin to bark out the Yiddish songs along with Hans. When I don't know the words, I make loud Yiddish-sounding noises. My crackly voice and my inability to carry a tune leave the audience holding their ears in disgust. Some of them stand up and walk out. One elderly man throws a piece of fruit at me, which I dodge without skipping a note. The Yiddish words gradually began to flow from me as though I've spoken the language my entire life. Hans puts his arm around my shoulder, and we sing until the gallery is empty, until our voices are the only sounds in the sleeping city.*

After the concert I walked around and looked at the exhibit. It had all the staples of the avant-garde art galleries I've occasionally stumbled upon in New York: a piece that depicted a graphic homosexual encounter; a collection of TVs stacked like bricks, playing video snippets you could watch for only about ten seconds without feeling insane; and the requisite mundane artifact hanging on a wall, in this case a pair of white soccer shorts, which Christine told me were the artist's statement on Austrian machismo.

Looking for someone to interview about the concert, I noticed a man in a blue jean jacket standing alone by the food table. He had wavy blond hair and sunken shoulders. I asked him if he had understood any parts of the songs.

"Yes," he said, "I understood about 90 percent. I grew up in the Austrian countryside. We have some dialects that are very similar to Yiddish."

I felt a rush of jealousy. I'm not sure if I believed the 90 percent line, but apparently, this non-Jewish Austrian had understood a lot more of the Yiddish than I had. It suddenly dawned on me that most German speakers, Nazis included, could understand the language of my grandparents better than I could.

"As an Austrian," I asked, "can you listen to Yiddish music as though it's just another type of music, or does it have special meaning in light of what happened in this country?"

The man looked annoyed by the question. "I was born in 1962, a long time after the war," he said. "I've heard a lot of things about concentration camps. Maybe I'm not close enough to it. But I've done nothing wrong. Maybe I'm free to listen to this music and to enjoy it. Sure, I think about the words. I've been to Israel to take a look around."

"So you don't think Austrians should focus on the country's past?"

"I think there has to be a point for all things," he said. "It's only been a couple of generations, but we should be far enough away to say, 'Okay, we can't change the past.' There has to be a point, just like with African blacks who were slaves in America or the American Indians. Sure, it's good to remember, but we have to look to the future, not only to the past."

I turned, and Hans was standing behind me.

"You found the right man," Hans said. "They have been telling us this for sixty years."

The man looked at Hans, then glanced at the ground. There was an awkward silence. I thanked him for the interview and walked away with Hans.

I was bothered by the encounter—not because I was offended, but because the man's arguments weren't all that easily dismissed. Although I remained firm in my belief that Austria had a long way to go before the country would be ready to move on, I hadn't stopped to think exactly what it would take to satisfy me. Certainly Austria can't mull over its war crimes forever. Vienna now had a beautiful memorial to Jewish victims of the Nazis; a new settlement had just been reached with the Jewish community on reparations for slave laborers; and the Austrian public schools now teach about the Holocaust and take students on trips to concentration camps. What, exactly, would the Austrians have to do before the country would be off the hook in my mind?

Hans put his hand on my arm and said there was someone he wanted me to meet. In the corner, sitting hunched on a stool, was a petite elderly woman with round glasses and short white hair.

"This is Ilse Aschner. She was in England during the war, like my father," Hans said. "When she came back, she worked at the Communist newspaper with my mother."

Several people standing by observed that I was interviewing Ilse and gathered around to listen. I asked her why she had come back to Austria after the war.

"I thought they were waiting for us to come home and build a new Austria," Ilse said. A few of the onlookers chuckled at the irony, but Ilse didn't seem to notice. "But I was wrong. Nobody wanted us. Nobody helped us find a job or a flat." The laughing stopped. "It wasn't about being Jewish or Communist. They just thought we were on the wrong side. They said to us, 'You've been on the side of the enemies.' There was this new 'we' feeling in the country, and the refugees who returned disturbed this."

I asked her if she regretted moving back to Austria.

"I've got family here and it's hard to move, but I've always been sorry that I left England. I don't feel at home here. Especially with the new government, I really feel it's not my country. My parents are Jewish, but I was baptized as a child. I went to a Protestant school. Yet I still feel the anti-Semitism, people clinging to Nazi thoughts."

Ilse's shaky voice was growing more firm.

"I talk to men of my generation, and they tell me how wonderful it was in the war and how great it was when they marched through Paris—what great adventures they had. Recently, I was talking to some people about anti-Semitism, and an old man came by and said, 'They forgot you, you should have gone into the gas too.' "

It was hard to imagine anyone saying something so awful to the tiny old woman sitting in front of me. This was my answer to the guy in the blue jean jacket, I thought. It doesn't matter how many symbolic gestures Austria makes. Austria can let go of its history when the symbolic gestures become more than symbols.

⌐‒‒‒

In the morning I had breakfast with Christine while Hans organized some of his things and showered. As I sipped my coffee, Christine showed me a book of photos of sculptures found in European cemeteries. The sculptures were of young lovers embracing, and some of them were fairly erotic.

Hans emerged from the bedroom in a gray V-neck that said YUTU on the left breast and a Nike JUST DO IT baseball cap. Knowing that Hans didn't buy his clothes so much as end up with them, I decided not to point out that Nike had become the embodiment of the capitalist ethic Hans had spent his entire life denouncing. Besides, "Just Do It" was a pretty good slogan for Hans.

Hans was taking me to meet his parents in a southern working-class district of Vienna. The Breuers still lived in the apartment where Hans grew up, part of a block of plain, white, four-story buildings separated by long rectangular lawns. The inside of the cramped two-bedroom was as modest as the building's exterior, the walls decorated only with framed photographs of the family. More photos were lined up across the top of the piano in the corner. In one of them, a twenty-something, bearded Hans is wearing a yellow hat that, amazingly, looks significantly larger than his current shepherd's hat.

There was no sign of Hans's parents. Hans led me into their bedroom and pointed to the cracks in the wooden floor.

"For years my father hurt his foot on this wood, but he would not spend money on himself to fix it," Hans said. "You see these values he gave me."

We stepped back into the living room, and Hans's mother, Rosa, emerged from the kitchen in a blue house-dress. She was solid and squat, barely five feet tall, with Hans's broad features and a helmet of fluffy white hair. She might have been a fullback on a football team of elderly midgets.

Rosa sat me down at the table in the center of the room, placed an unsolicited egg in front of me, then disappeared back into the kitchen. The egg had its own stand, and I spent the next few minutes unsure of how to eat it, until Hans ("I see you do not know how to eat soft egg") leaned over and cracked the top for me.

A few minutes later Georg walked into the apartment in a white undershirt and blue shorts that looked uncomfortably small. His exposed limbs were skinny and draped in sagging flesh. His hair had receded to the back of his head, where it grew unruly, making him look a bit like a less rotund David Ben-Gurion. Additional small tufts of gray hair gathered like tumbleweed in his ears.

Georg said hello to me and sat down to my right. It wasn't clear that he knew who I was. He turned to Hans and told him that someone in the building wanted to buy a lamb from him. Hans wrote down the customer's name and phone number in a notebook—momentarily seeming like a normal businessman—then explained that I wanted to do an inter-view.

Ever since Hans had given me the outline of Georg's story during our initial conversation in New York, I had wondered why Georg had chosen to come back to Austria after the war. The product of a middle-class and very assimilated Viennese Jewish family, Georg was studying to become a symphony conductor until politics and then the Nazis got in the way. After the Austrian fascists took control of the government in 1934, Georg, then fifteen, felt obliged to do something. He founded a leftist activist group with friends at school and began planning actions along with the Communist Youth. In 1936 the police showed up at Georg's school and threw him in jail for a month. Two years later, just weeks before the Nazis arrived in Vienna, Georg fled to Switzerland, worried more about his political ties than about being Jewish. After a year in Switzerland, he joined his parents in England, where, along with other refugees who held German and Austrian passports, he was declared an "enemy alien" and sent to an internment camp for six months. With the end of the war in 1945, Georg returned home with dreams of rebuilding a new Communist Austria.

"If it's okay, I'd like to ask some questions," I said. Hans left the room to talk with his mother in the kitchen.

"Fine," Georg said, "but first I would like to ask you a question. What do you think of your country's nuclear policy?"

"Um, I'm not sure," I said.

Georg stood up, walked to his bedroom, and returned with a fact sheet on recent U.S. violations of various nuclear treaties. "It's hard to believe what your president is doing," he said. He had a German accent and the raspy voice of an old man, but his English was fairly good.

"Yes," I said. "So can I ask why you came back to Austria after the war? Weren't you angry at the country?"

Georg smiled, as though it were an absurd question. "Was I angry at the country? You know, there were different people in Austria," he said. "Not everybody was a Nazi, of course. And my mother and I came back because neither she nor I was prepared to accept that some nationalistic idiots could say that we are not Austrians. We are."

"And you've never regretted the decision to return?"

"You see, I am angry about Nazis and anti-Semites," Georg said. "I am angry about the way the government since 1945 has been handling this—not because they were anti-Semitic, but because they were afraid of losing votes. But I am not angry about the Austrians because this is not a clear-cut case, and I think the general trend is rather positive. Comparing the time when I first came back with today, I would say there are fewer anti-Semites. Fewer Nazis."

"But when I think about how the Austrians accepted the Nazis . . ."

Georg made a face like he had just swallowed a little too much horseradish. "It is not true that the Austrian people as a whole were Nazis. This is not true," he said. "There should have been a vote in Austria in March of 1938 about whether Austria would become part of Germany."

"But there was a vote, and 99 percent—"

"That's not true! Hitler marched in to prevent the real vote, and then there was this fake ballot you mention. I am not sure whether the majority was pro or con, but Hitler wasn't sure either."

The "real vote" Georg was referring to was an initiative of the Christian Social fascist leader Kurt von Schuschnigg. In February 1938, even before the Germans arrived, the Austrian Nazis were taking control of one Austrian city after another. On March 9, 1938, in a desperate last effort to maintain his country's independence, Schuschnigg called for an emergency plebiscite. Austrians were to go to the polls on March 13 to determine if Austria was to remain an independent nation or unite with Germany. Hitler, having already decided to include Austria in the German Reich, was outraged at Schuschnigg's last-minute attempt to derail the process. Two days later German troops were in Vienna. The next month the Nazis held their own plebiscite on the unification, and, at least according to the Nazis, 99.73 percent of Austrians had voted in favor of Austria becoming a part of the Reich. Scholars have since called the number into question, but few dispute that a great majority voted for the Nazis.

Hans had warned me that Georg was an unshakable optimist, but even so, I was surprised. Georg had had a nearly identical experience to that of Ilse Aschner, the woman I had spoken with after Hans's performance at the gallery. And yet they seemed to see the postwar Austrian experience in almost opposite lights.

I wasn't sure what to make of it. I had been in Austria for weeks, waiting patiently for that instant when all of the conflicting stories I had heard would come together in one blaringly clear conclusion. But with each day I was growing more rather than less confused.

I shifted directions and asked Georg how he felt about Hans having left home at the age of fifteen to join Spartakus.

Georg let out a long sigh. "I was just glad he didn't become a terrorist," he said.

"A terrorist?"

"You were too young to experience 1968. It was not that

I thought Hansie in particular would be a terrorist, but there was general trend of youth revolt at the time, and thousands of young people did things which in other times they wouldn't have done. Terrorism was only one part of that trend, but I don't think any parent at that time could say, 'My son will not do that.'" Georg paused and gave me a "Just wait until you figure out what life is really like" look. "There was this feeling that the world is awful," he continued, "but I think their response was largely exaggerated compared with the world I have experienced and that my wife experienced under Hitler's rule. At least in sixty-eight, Austria was a democratic country. It was much better than the past we had known—not the most terrible of all worlds you can think of."

Later I sat down with Rosa. With Hans translating, she recounted her capture by the Gestapo. I hardly spoke as she made her way through the story. Rosa kept her hands in her lap. She seemed at ease, if serious. Hans, by contrast, maintained a pained expression throughout the interview.

When Rosa told me about her suicide attempt at the Gestapo headquarters, she leaned forward and parted her hair with her hands.

"She wants you should see her scar," Hans said.

I looked. A long curving line like a faded chalk mark ran across the top of her head.

When the story was over, we took a break. Rosa brought me toast, and Hans showed me some of the buttons he had saved from his early teens. They were mostly in English and almost laughably representative of the times: STOP U.S. AGGRESSION IN VIETNAM, FREEDOM NOW, JESUS WORE LONG HAIR, BABY I AM SINGLE, ALL I NEED IS LOVE.

Next Hans took out a handful of old photos. In one, a twelve-year-old, chubby-cheeked Hans is standing at an anti–nuclear proliferation rally organized by Georg in black-rimmed glasses, a small cap, and a jacket with a white-painted peace symbol on the front. Around him people are holding umbrellas, looking up at a speaker, but Hans stands unprotected in the rain, staring off to the side, his face a study in glumness. I wouldn't have imagined there was a photo that could have better summed up Hans's childhood, but Hans produced another picture from 1965 of him at a memorial for an elderly Communist who was beaten to death by a neo-Nazi student, the first person killed by a Nazi in Austria after the war. In the crowd of the fifty or so people who are visible in the photo, Hans is the only child. His face is dead serious.

"I was deenosaurus," Hans said, looking at the photo.
"Dinosaur?"
"Yes, yes," Hans said. "During these years I was like generation of my parents, only talking with people much older than me. They would look at me and say, 'He is young, but already he has so many sorrows.' "

# Twenty-three

# Seeds of Fascism

She had blond hair down to the small of her back and a small mouth. Hans wanted her and she wanted him. They moved closer together on the bed. Hans put his arm around her.

"I don't even know your name," she said.

Hans told her.

"You're 'the Breuer' Remi talks about?" The woman looked like she had just seen a ghost. She jumped out of the bed. "I'm sorry," she said.

The woman's refusal to sleep with him was as clear a sign as Hans could ask for that there was no chance for him to ever be happy at Longo Maï. "She let me fall like hot potatoes," Hans told me. "I understood from this that I had to leave this place."

Not that the encounter with the woman was the only incident that had led Hans to rethink his commitment to Longo Maï. There was also the accident at the wool-spinning shop, when a member of the community had gotten his arm stuck on a lever and was slowly being sucked into a machine: "I watched these so-called partisans stand paralyzed as this man was being killed, and I started to see that all this talk of taking action is lies," Hans said. And then there was the day Hans had been sick with a high fever and unable to work: Remi told him that he was fine, that people who work outdoors have higher temperatures. Hans protested and turned to another member of the group standing nearby. "Tell him it's not true," Hans had said. The man looked at Hans and then at "the Great Educator." "It's true what Remi tells you," the man said.

"Remi could say, 'This is a black world' when the world is white, and everybody would agree," Hans told me. "So I saw a little bit there how people participate in a fascist system and don't see what they're doing. They create their own inner world, where what's right and wrong can be changed by the group. It becomes possible that collective crimes are done without people feeling guilty."

Hans had come full circle. He had joined Spartakus to fight fascism only to discover the seeds of fascism within the group. But no matter how miserable he was at Longo Maï, leaving wasn't easy. For months Hans had been changing his mind, and just the thought of cutting himself off from the community could cause him to break into a sweat. Then there were the logistical problems to tackle: He had no money and no property of his own—to take even a rucksack would be to steal from the collective; he would have to make it by the guards and the packs of roaming dogs Remi had in-stalled, supposedly to keep the enemies out, but, Hans was discovering, really to keep the residents of Longo Maï in.

Weeks after his encounter with the woman, Hans stood by himself at three in the morning and thought about the look on her face when he had revealed his name. Then he grabbed a rucksack and headed into the night. After slip-ping by the guards and making his way through several thorny fields, Hans arrived at a road where he could hail a ride in the direction of Austria. When he had made it several hours away, Hans still felt Longo Maï's grip. He got out of the car that had picked him up and found a phone to call the community. The phone was passed to Remi, who told Hans that a car would be sent to pick him up and bring him back. Hans thought hard about it, then stuck out his thumb and caught another car in the direction of Vienna. "Even then," Hans told me, "I was convinced that it was my defeat—not that the place was bad, but that I was bad."

# Twenty-four

# The Caravan

From his childhood home, Hans and I drove to his "caravan," as he called it, which was parked in Gaming, another absurdly picturesque Austrian town. Back in the blue van, the shepherd's sticks poking me in the back, the smell of the sheep calling up memories of my lamb-herding days, I asked Hans to once again try to explain why he hadn't immediately left Longo Maï. "Couldn't you see how crazy it was?" I asked.

"Maybe a little," Hans said, his face filled with the same sadness I had first noticed at his concert in New York. "But the world outside of the group seemed crazy to me too."

Hans looked at me just long enough to make me fear he was going to crash the van. "And it was not only bad things there," he continued. "Not everybody was like Remi. There were some very peaceful people who were not part of this system. It was mixed with a lot of mess, but we were not foolish in all respects. And what I'm doing today—these ideas come from the group. Now I'm always looking for people to sing with, but there I just had to start to sing and some people would join with me. And I don't regret that I was there. It was important time for me because I learned that you can invent new things based on old traditions, like being shepherd."

I had almost forgotten. If there had been no Longo Maï, there would have been no introduction into the world of shepherding. Hans had told me that although he had sheared the sheep at Longo Maï, he had never been allowed to be a shepherd. The sheep held a special status in the community as a symbol of the group's return to a more peaceful way of life, and Hans was simply not high enough in the Longo Maï hierarchy to have the honor of leading the flock. Mostly Hans worked at office jobs, which he hated, or in the wood shop making tables, which he loved. But he remembers standing and watching the shepherds from a distance and wanting badly to join them.

Hans, I realized, had lived in perhaps the only place in the world where being a shepherd was the ultimate status symbol, where would-be shepherds were denied the privilege of carrying the stick. Hans never put it this way, but it seems that by becoming a shepherd, he was, at least in part, making a statement to the residents of Longo Maï.

The caravan where Hans, Kati, and their three sons had lived for a good portion of the last decade was parked for the moment on the property of a one-handed hunter named Wolfgang Pikl (pronounced Pickle). Hans pays only a token sum in rent, but he also gives Wolfgang Pikl lamb meat from time to time. I remembered that Hans had given lamb meat to Manfred as well, and it occurred to me that he was trading with a currency that had probably been out of use for a good 2,000 years.

Set in the shade of a small patch of woods, the brown caravan was the size of a modest mobile home and had a thick metal hitch on the front so that Hans could pull it with the van—which he does several times a year, depending on the location of the flock.

I stepped inside the caravan. To my right was the kitchen: a freestanding woodstove, a counter, and a breakfast table, above which a poster of smiling South American children was taped. To my left was a tiny bedroom, where three sets of bunk beds lined the three walls. Hans had placed a board across the two parallel bottom bunks, so that they functioned as what looked like an extremely uncomfortable queen bed. It was parents on bottom, kids on top.

And that was it. Maybe six steps of clear walking space in the whole home.

"It's hard to imagine five people living in there," I said to Hans as we stepped back outside.

"Yes, and sometimes guests too," Hans said. "But we are outside with sheep most times, and this was like luxury compared to old caravan." Hans pointed to a white trailer parked about twenty yards away that was about half the size of the caravan I had just been in. Hans told me that Andi now lived in the small caravan by himself and that he had his own TV and PlayStation in there.

By then I knew the important question to ask: "How did you and Kati manage to have sex with the kids sleeping in bunk beds on top of you?"

"It was okay," Hans said. "When Andi and Günter were younger, they would hear a little bit and they made up name for it: 'wackypoki.' It was funny for them. They would write little comics and things like this."

"What about a bathroom?"

Hans led me around the back of the caravan and pointed to a bucket. "When you are done, you cover it with some ashes and there is no smell," he said seeming genuinely proud. "This is old custom I learned from the Roma."

Hans pointed to a clump of trees. "Over there was where we once had the foosball table," he said, explaining how he and Kati had bought the table for the boys to reward their hard work with the sheep.

With that, Hans climbed up a rusty ladder attached to the back of the caravan and began to sweep the leaves off the roof. I walked over to the smaller caravan to take a look. It was only slightly larger than a van. There was hardly space for one person to move, but Hans and Kati had lived there for years with two sons: the parents on one bed, Günter on the other, and Andi sleeping on the floor with his legs tucked under Günter's bed.

Standing erect, my head nearly grazed the ceiling, so I lay down and thought about Hans's life from this new perspective. There was no longer room for romanticizing. The guy was living in worse conditions than most third-world refugees.

I fell asleep and awoke to the sight of Hans grinning at me through the caravan's window. When I stepped outside,

Hans announced that he had had many passionate moments
in the bed I was sleeping in.

Before leaving, Hans wanted to show me how the family
bathed when they stayed on the Pikl property. He led me to
a carved-out log about twenty yards away from the caravan
that was filled with water that didn't look particularly clean.

"Touch it," Hans said.

The water was ice-cold.

Hans stripped naked and jumped into the log.

I looked nervously at the son of Wolfgang Pikl kicking a
soccer ball nearby. Hans stepped out of the log and got
dressed. It was time to go.

# Twenty-five

# Caravan of Dreams

I come back into the caravan all wet. Irene is sitting at the table. She is mad.

"Did you just bathe in the log again?" she asks.

"Yes," I say. "I just bathed in the log again."

"That water is filthy," Irene says.

"I know," I say.

Irene stands up and steps into the bedroom. "I can't live here anymore," she says.

"Live where?" I ask.

"Here," she says. "In Wolfgang Pikl's backyard."

"But this was your idea," I say. "Remember? We would smoke and be in love and nothing else would matter. . . ."

"Yes, but that was before you started with the Jew-ish thing."

*Irene is referring to my recently developed habit of point-
ing to my chest and repeatedly blurting out the word "Jewish"—not "I am Jewish," not "I'm a Jew," just the two
vowelly syllables: "Jew-ish." Last night it had happened during dinner. Irene asked me to pass the salt, and out of nowhere
I hit her with three straight: "Jew-ish, Jew-ish, Jew-ish."*

"I would stop if I could," I say.

"So just stop," she says.

"I said I would if I could," I say.

*Irene opens the door. I ask her where she's going.*

"Where do you think?" she says.

"To play foosball with that Russian shoeshine guy," I
say.

"Right," she says.

"Mr. 'There are more Nazis in America than here,' " I
say.

"He's a nice guy," Irene says.

"He's a bastard," I say. "He's probably not even Jewish.
The Russians used to pretend to be Jewish to get out of the
country."

"Whatever," Irene says. *She steps out.*

"Do you want to have sex in the woods?" I call.

*Irene closes the door behind her. I am alone. I knock on
Wolfgang Pikl's door but no one answers, and so I just start
walking. I walk for hours. The sky goes from blue to orange to
red to gray. I am tired, but I don't stop until I come upon a tall
man standing in a yellow field. The man is holding a giant
scythe.*

"Hallo," I say.

"Hallo," *he says.*

"I'm Sam," I say.

"I'm Death," he says.

"Mind if I ask you a question?" I say.

"Bitte," Death says.

"Is it my turn?" I ask. I am strangely calm.

"Nope," Death says.

"Could you tell me when?" I ask. "It would, ya know, save me a lot of worrying time."

"No can do," Death says.

"Do I have rabies?" I ask.

"How the hell should I know?" Death says. "Why do you worry so much?"

"Jew-ish," I say, my thumb aimed at my chest.

Death looks at me like I'm crazy.

"Jew-ish Jew-ish," I say.

## Twenty-six

# In the Army Tent

Later that week Irene and I went to the annual outdoors festival held on Vienna's Danube canal. The air smelled of grilled animal flesh, and as soon as we arrived, I felt overwhelmed by the swarms of Viennese teenagers. They were dancing and typing messages into their cell phones and whipping one another with rolled-up T-shirts. Some of them wore lit-up devil horns.

I immediately sought out a stand selling roasted corn on the cob, because I generally find these roasted-corn stands to be the only unambiguously redeeming thing about outdoor festivals.

Irene bought a drink, and we sat down at a picnic table. I told her that I would have to leave Vienna in a few days and that it was going to be hard to say good-bye.

She smiled but didn't say anything. It made me nervous. I picked a few kernels of corn from my teeth. We walked on until we came across a large canvas tent that was closed on all sides.

"It's a tent of the army," Irene said. "They're making exhibits at the festival during the day."

We looked at each other, then walked to the front of the tent, unzipped the flap, and went inside.

It was pitch-dark and peaceful, the noise of the crowd now an even hum. Irene sat down and took out one of her lighters. Her face flickered in the light. I stretched out with my head in her lap and asked her to be careful not to burn my hair.

"I've never met anyone who worries so much about things like this," Irene said.

"Okay, um, please just try not to burn my hair," I said. Then I began to sing songs from the musical *Hair*.

Irene impressed me by knowing most of the words. When we had done every *Hair* song we knew, Irene taught me a German protest song, and we sang it together softly:

*Hey ho, leistet Widerstand*
*Gegen den Rassismus in dem Land*
*Schliesst euch fest zusammmen,*
*Schliesst euch fest zusammmen.*

Hey ho, resist
The racism in this country
Firmly join your forces,
Firmly join your forces.

"I think I'm really starting to like you," Irene said, her fingers pressing on the sides of my neck.

I felt nervous again. I was really starting to like her too. What I hadn't understood about the "travel relationship" before I left for Austria is that it makes things much harder rather than easier. Had Irene and I both lived in the same city, I probably would have been fixating on how different our personalities were. But the travel relationship allows you to put down your guard, to slip seamlessly into feelings you would otherwise keep at bay. And then, just like that, just when your heart is fully exposed, it's time to get on a plane and go.

I tried to deflect the tension with a joke. "Oh, come on, you just have some sort of thing for Jewish guys," I said, temporarily forgetting that I had already been scolded for this exact remark a few days earlier.

Irene's voice lost its softness.

"Trust me," she said, "I don't have a special thing for Jewish guys."

Then she stood up and walked out of the tent.

I followed her out. "I'm sorry," I said. "I was just joking around."

"It's nothing," Irene said. "I'm sorry."

We sat down and watched the teenagers sing karaoke. Two boys were doing "Summer Lovin'" from *Grease* as their friends cheered them on.

I picked more kernels of corn from my teeth. Irene rolled a joint.

"A Jewish guy tried to rape me when I was sixteen," she said.

"Jesus," I said.

Holding hands, we left the festival and walked to a party a friend of Irene's was throwing. I felt sad for Irene and angry at myself for having raised the subject again. I couldn't help thinking about what was going through that rapist's head. Probably he was just cruel and demented in the way all rapists are cruel and demented, but maybe he had been caught up in his own psychosexual drama about Austria and the Jews. Maybe he had really been after Austria more than Irene.

I felt sick.

The party was in a large apartment full of computers and ashtrays and plastic cups that had been abandoned mid-drink. A dark-skinned man with long hair strummed a guitar in the corner.

I sat on the living room couch between Irene and a girl whose short blond hair looked as though it hadn't been washed in a long time. I asked her what she did, and she said, "Nothing." Then she said that she wanted to be a doctor but that she couldn't be one in Austria.

Across from me a pregnant woman was taking a hit from a joint.

"Why not?" I asked.

"You must not have heard about Dr. Gross," she said.

"No," I said, and then she told me the story. Until the late 1990s, Dr. Gross had been one of Austria's leading neurologists, regularly giving expert testimony in court. During World War II he had worked in the Am Spiegelgrund clinic, which is now part of the Vienna State Psychiatric Hospital. Despite his denials, there is considerable evidence that while working at the clinic, Dr. Gross supervised cruel experiments on physically and mentally disabled children—both Jews and Gentiles—whom the Nazis called *lebensunwertes Leben*, or "life unworthy of life." When the doctors were done with the children, they killed them with barbiturates and put their brains in jars that were kept in the basement of the clinic and used for research as recently as 1998.

That almost 800 children were killed in the Am Spiegelgrund clinic was no secret. The director, Emst Illing, was hanged as a war criminal in 1945. Gross was tried and convicted on one count of manslaughter in 1950, but, as was typical of Austrian Nazi trials, his conviction was overturned on a technicality after only a few months. Dr. Gross went back to work and personally continued to experiment on the brains of the murdered children well into the mid-1960s. In 1975 the Austrian government presented him with a high state medal for his services to the country.

A new attempt to prosecute Gross on nine counts of murder began again in 1999, after a researcher found medical notes Gross had taken in the summer of 1944 in a Berlin archive. It would have been Austria's first Nazi war crimes trial in a quarter of a century, but it was suspended after a court ruled that Dr. Gross suffered from dementia.

The children's brains were finally buried in April of 2002.

From the party we went back to the two-bedroom apartment Irene shared with her roommate, Dani. The apartment was full of what Irene referred to as her "inventions": The remote control was attached to the futon mattress on the floor by an elastic cord; the bookcase doubled as a stairway up to her loft. The bathtub was in the kitchen, and Irene mentioned that she sometimes did dishes while she showered. In the bathroom Irene had posted cartoons and newspapers clippings. One of the banners read: ÖSTERREICH IST KEIN NAZI-LAND ("Austria is not a Nazi country"). I asked her why it was there, and she said that she thought it was funny that the newspaper had felt the need to run the statement as a headline.

We undressed and climbed onto the loft in Irene's bedroom. I had a bunch of small stickers that came with my blank audiocassettes, and I put them on Irene's feet. Then I apologized again for my comment about her liking Jewish guys.

"Forget about it," she said.

I tried, but I couldn't.

# Twenty-seven

# The Shepherd
# of Vienna

Four days after leaving Longo Maï, Hans arrived at his parents' apartment. He had no friends, no job skills, and no idea what to do next. He stayed in his parent's flat for three weeks until his father, Georg, came up with a plan. Georg had inherited a small estate outside of Vienna, where Hans's grandfather had run a vegetarian pension from 1930 to 1938. The property had been neglected for years, and Georg offered to pay Hans to clear some of the dead trees around the house. Hans, still struggling to readjust to life outside of Longo Maï, found the logging cathartic. He continued to clear trees through the winter of 1975. In the spring he began traveling around Austria, working odd jobs as a farmhand and falling in love with teenage girls. The next winter Hans cut down trees again. Then, on April 1, Rosa saw an ad in the newspaper: The city of Vienna was looking for a shepherd.

"Everyone thought it was April joke," Hans said.

It was no joke. The city owned a lot of unused land, and someone in the bureaucracy came up with the idea of putting a flock of sheep on a few of the fields so that they would not go to waste. Rosa pushed hard for Hans to apply. As a city worker, he would receive a good wage, a cheap apartment, and a measure of job security. "My mother wanted I would be pragmaticized," Hans said, unable to hold back his laughter.

Hans got the job by exaggerating here and there about the extent of his experience working with sheep. "I had really not much idea of what it is to be shepherd," he said, "but we say among the blind ones, the one-eyed is king."

As it turned out, Hans was not only "one-eyed," but also one-legged, having recently broken his leg in two places after an ill-fated attempt at bareback horse riding. In those first months as the shepherd of Vienna, he would limp along with his stick, taking sixty sheep back and forth through a stretch of woods to a grazing patch without even a dog to help him.

Hans liked the sheep but hated dealing with the city bureaucrats. Every time a ewe fell sick, he would have to place a written request to buy medicine. By the time he received a response, it would often be too late. Meanwhile, the bureaucrats began to catch on that Hans didn't know much about shepherding. After some months the city sent him off to shepherd's school in West Germany for three weeks to learn from the experts. Hans took the same courses as the other shepherds, but because he didn't have the requisite nine years of experience working with sheep, he wasn't able to get what he referred to as his "master's of shepherding."

To get a master's in shepherding, you have to take a final exam: The shepherd is given a flock of 500 sheep, which he has to lead over a bridge with his dogs standing on either side until the last sheep has passed. No lamb herders are allowed at the back. The shepherd also has to take the sheep into the streets amid traffic and then drive them back into a fenced-off grazing area. "If the dog does not do things just right, then you can go home," Hans said.

There is also a written test with a wide range of questions about sheep and the finances of keeping a flock. "They will ask you: If you have a flock of one thousand sheep, how much food will you need for the winter?" Hans explained. "And if you start to tell some numbers, then again you can go home because you first must ask in what region the flock is and how much energy they get from the food there and so on."

Like a lot of good schools, the shepherd's academy turned out to be as useful for the connections you could make as for its curriculum. While there, Hans met a handful of shepherds from an alternative community in southwest Germany called Finkhof—a much less radical version of Longo Maï. The Finkhof community had several shepherds with degrees, and later these Finkhof shepherds would be the ones to really teach Hans the secrets of the trade.

After his schooling, Hans went back to Vienna and continued to herd the city sheep. He brought his first dogs back from Germany and began to train them. But having seen real

German shepherds in action, Hans found his daily routine of leading his sheep back and forth within the same small area even less appealing.

The dissatisfaction was heightened by Hans's loneliness. For all its many drawbacks, Longo Maï had provided Hans with a community that was now entirely absent from his life. And making new friends was hard. Hans was still a radical and still largely incapable of getting along with anyone who didn't share his extreme opinions—which was almost everyone. "I fought with everyone like they were enemies, only now I see that they were not enemies, only critical friends," Hans said.

Whenever he had a chance, Hans visited his friends at Finkhof, and with each trip, he grew more impressed with the young shepherds in the community. It wasn't just the way the Finkhof shepherds kept perfect control over the flock—although that certainly excited Hans; it was the way they had integrated their sheep into the life of the countryside.

Finkhof's flock wandered through Upper Swabia, a stretch of gentle foothills in southern Germany known for its mild winters and lean grasslands. For centuries the countryside had been maintained by grazing sheep, but as small-scale village shepherding disappeared over the decades, the green pastures and riverbanks in the region had been overtaken by shrubbery and weeds. The Finkhof shepherds had an idea: They approached the local officials and arranged to bring sheep back to the region as makeshift lawn mowers. For the shepherds it would mean a small wage and free food for the flock. For the local officials it would be a cheap and environmentally friendly way to keep the countryside beautiful. The Finkhof shepherds made similar arrangements with farmers in the area. In the late autumn, when the crops had been harvested, the sheep could move onto the farmers' fields and eat the leftover leaves and seedlings. For the shepherd it was again free food. For the farmer it was old-fashioned weeding and fertilizer. The great insight was that the same voracious sheep appetite that made it so tricky to keep a flock near other people's property could be a valuable tool if properly harnessed. (The urban equivalent of this idea, which I wholeheartedly endorse, would be to have large herds of goats replace our current trash-collecting system.)

As Hans too came to appreciate the social and economic potential in sheep hunger, the shepherding life took on a great new appeal for him. By eating what would otherwise go to waste, the sheep were making the world more efficient and allowing Hans to stay true to his Marxist roots. If he followed the Finkhof model, he would own no property and monopolize no resources. And, even better, since Hans had no money, this system required almost no investment once a shepherd had some sheep—there was no need even to buy hay. But perhaps best of all, considering that Hans was still having a hard time getting along with just about everyone and still capable of seeing capitalist corruption and fascism just about everywhere, the job of a wandering shepherd would isolate him from the rest of society.

Hans thought about moving to Finkhof to become a shepherd in Germany. But Finkhof already had more than enough shepherds. Hans wondered if he could bring the Finkhof system back to Austria, but it didn't seem likely. He would need to find a place that had both little snowfall in winter (sheep, according to Hans, will dig through only about forty centimeters of snow), plenty of unused land, and local officials who had a bit of imagination.

Hans didn't realize such a place might exist in Austria until the winter of 1979, when two young women from the Lower Austrian town of Krems came to visit Hans at Finkhof. They mentioned that not far from where they lived were overgrown pastures just like ones grazed by the Finkhof sheep and that the Danube valley that spreads across Lower Austria also has microclimates with little snowfall—due to the mixing of the Mediterranean climate from the south and the Continental climate from the east. The two women even volunteered to ask local officials how they would feel about Hans bringing a flock to the area.

Hans was thrilled. The prospect of being a wandering shepherd in Austria seemed suddenly close at hand. But before he took the next monumental step, he wanted to go to Scandinavia. Remi had always talked about Scandinavia as a place where the people were more open-minded and less sexually repressed, and Hans wanted to check this out for himself. He never imagined he would begin to discover his Jewish heritage on the journey.

Twenty-eight

# Everybody Knows in Which Echo I Write

In less than a week I was scheduled to leave for Israel, where I was going to visit my sister and her family. On my way home to New York, I would stop over in Vienna for one night. That was it. I had entered another world of sheep, sex, and Nazis, and just like that, it would be gone.

The morning after the festival I interviewed Doron Rabinovici, a well-known Austrian Jewish writer who has explored the theme of Jewish life in Austria in both his fiction and nonfiction. Rabinovici is also a prominent political activist and had helped to organize the huge protests that filled the streets of Vienna in the days after the new government had formed. Prior to my trip, when I asked around for names of people to talk to about the Jewish experience in Austria, Rabinovici was usually the first person mentioned.

I arrived at the café where Rabinovici had suggested we meet to find him already sitting at a table sipping coffee and reading the newspaper. He was thin, with close-cropped brown hair and small black-framed glasses that gave him the air of a cutting-edge intellectual, the kind of guy you suspected of writing academic jargon in the margins of nonacademic books.

Rabinovici told me that he had moved to Vienna from Tel Aviv when he was three. Both of his parents were Holocaust survivors, and he had grown up with the sense that the past wasn't really over, that what happened between 1938 and 1945 could happen again. He sounded like Hans, but, unlike Hans, Rabinovici had always had a strong Jewish identity and been active in Zionist youth groups.

"In Vienna, I was very aware of Jewish questions in a way that I maybe would not have been in Tel Aviv, and quite certainly not in New York," Rabinovici said, his eyes intense. "In other big cities, you live in the Diaspora, but there's still a large Jewish community—you're not 'you people.' In Vienna you're always some kind of last member of a murdered people." Rabinovici looked down into his coffee, then back up at me. "To be a Jew in Austria after the war and not feel that you are a Jew would be very, very strange," he said.

I asked Rabinovici how living in Vienna affected his fiction.

"Just to write as a Jew in a German-speaking country—in a country where once the National Socialists were in power—is always a contradiction to what the murderers wanted," he said. "And even more so, to write as a Jew in

German." He thought for a moment. "I would maybe say that what I'm doing is indirect or second-degree writing. I can write a novel or a history work or an article, but it's indirect in a sense because what I do is always a reaction. When I write about a tree, I don't write only about a tree. And when I write about the Jewish child dancing in the street, I don't write only about the Jewish child dancing in the street because everybody knows in which echo I write. In the eyes of the murderers, Jews in Austria are people who should not exist. And in the moment when you open a book by such a person, you're aware of it and read it in a different way."

"It seems so confining," I said.

"Yes, but it's not just a restraint, it's also a possibility," Rabinovici said. "There was a great pianist who had a disease that affected his fingers and made his playing different, made something special about it. So someone like this might have limitations, but maybe there are things he can do better. He has possibilities other people don't have. The moment when you accept that, you can tell more stories. That's the interesting thing. If you don't accept it, you're more restricted. If you accept it, you can go on."

Rabinovici and I continued to talk for some time, about Haider and Austrian racism, but from the moment he had mentioned the inescapability of a Jewish identity in postwar Austria, my thoughts kept drifting back to Irene and the rapist. It struck me that she thought of him not just as a rapist, but as a Jewish rapist. I wondered if Irene was any more capable of seeing me outside of a Jewish context than I was capable of seeing her outside of an Austrian context. Maybe we were both hopelessly trapped in the past?

Before leaving, I asked Rabinovici if he ever felt worn-out by the ongoing struggle against anti-Semitism and racism in Austria.

"Well, I don't think you stay here because you have to fulfill a duty," he said. "But if you stay here, then you have to fight anti-Semitism. It's not that I'm staying here to fight, but if I stay here, I fight."

Later that day Irene and I biked along the banks of the Danube to a nudist swimming spot. I had understood that people would be swimming naked in the lake, but I hadn't anticipated that everyone would be hanging around without clothes even out of the water. Everywhere I turned there was flesh: naked kids kicking soccer balls and naked old men riding bicycles and naked families eating ice-cream cones together at picnic tables.

I had never seen so many naked people before, and I didn't particularly like it. I had always imagined a nude beach as some sort of erotic wonderland. Hairy old men on bikes, their large guts sagging over their shriveled dicks, had not been a part of that vision.

Irene and I arrived and put out a blanket on the grass. She took off her clothes and wrapped herself in a small Tibetan tapestry. "It's okay, you can undress," she said.

"No thanks," I said.

"Are you sure?" Irene asked, removing a box of cherries from her bag.

I was sure. I didn't want to be naked in front of the Viennese.

"Don't worry about me," I said. "I'll be fine."

"Do you like swimming?" Irene asked.

"Not really," I said. I have always been a terrible swimmer—I suspect because, deep down, I can never fully convince myself that I'm not going to drown each time I put my face in the water.

Irene leaned back on her elbows and ate cherries. I couldn't stop thinking about Rabinovici's dancing children, about Jewish echoes. I wanted to say something but I was worried she'd get upset again. Instead I asked her how she thought Austria's past affected her personally, if there was a link between the Nazi years and all of the work she did on behalf of refugees in the country.

"My father and aunt were both sent to Nazi schools," she said, "and my grandfather was away in Poland during the war. My family told me lots of stories—some I didn't believe and still don't, but I've started to understand the pressure they were under." Irene took a joint out of her bag and lit it. "I was still in the generation in which you weren't allowed to speak about that 'special chapter in Austrian history' with your family, so I was only told about the horror of the U.S. bombs and the lack of food. When I learned in school about the Holocaust and then visited Mauthausen, it really touched me deeply. It was a new version of history, like falling out of a warm, cozy cloud. So then I was confronted with trusting my family again. There were so many questions, like 'Why didn't you do anything?' and 'Don't you feel guilty?'—questions I never got an answer to. I still think that my grandfather, who died before I was born, had some secrets. I don't know what he did in Poland or Russia. Maybe I'm just being paranoid, since I didn't find anything about him when I looked up his name. It's just a feeling." She exhaled a plume of smoke. "I think I somehow just don't want to look away when I feel that there is injustice," she said.

We walked to the edge of the lake, where I removed my shirt, socks, and shoes. Irene removed her tapestry and led me across the lake to a rope swing that hung from a high branch overlooking the water. "Watch," she said. She climbed out of the lake onto a lower branch and took the rope in her hands. Then she swung, naked, limbs cascading through the air, and down beneath the water. Seconds later she reemerged with a "Whooo."

Irene wanted me to swing too. I thought hard. I was worried that I would let go before I made it over the water. Surely it happened sometimes, especially to people who were nervous and had sweaty palms. (CLOTHED TOURIST DIES AT NUDE LAKE: PAGE 5.) But it also looked sort of fun, and Irene was pressuring me. I climbed onto the branch, squeezed the rope in my fists, and swung. When I made it over the water, I dropped straight down, arms at my sides.

"Do you want to go again?" Irene said.

"Let's have a swimming race," I said.

We raced. I kicked and clawed at the water as hard as I could, but Irene beat me soundly.

On our way out Irene bumped into an old friend, an anarchist with one lazy eye and bad teeth. We ended up in a long argument about moral relativism. He seemed to be all for it. I said, "What if Irene suddenly stood up and for no reason kicked me in the face? Would that be an inherently wrong act?"

"Well, it would certainly be surprising," he said.

Over the next few days I tracked down some of Hans's old friends. Several former members of Spartakus and Longo Maï told me about the inner workings of the community, but they seemed guarded in talking about Hans. The most I could get out of them was that he was very active and never very happy.

A friend from high school who had been in the same section of the Communist Youth as Hans but hadn't joined Spartakus told me that he thought the entire Spartakus gang was crazy.

"Because they were so extreme?" I asked.

"No, I was very extreme myself."

"You mean really crazy?"

"Yes. Insane."

"Hans too?"

"I'm not sure," he said.

I asked another friend, Renate, who had been an important confidante for Hans during his worst ups and downs with Kati, if she had any understanding of the role foosball played in the family.

"I don't know," she said. "I only knew that it was very important for Kati and certainly that it gave her a simple and entertaining leisure activity away from Hans and away from discussing things. She could meet people who also just wanted to have fun."

Hans's younger sister, Lisi, initially agreed to talk to me, then changed her mind. She and Hans haven't spoken in years, but they are close with each other's children. As far as I could gather, the problem stemmed from their childhoods.

Hans and Lisi had been extremely close, but Hans was always a domineering figure. When he moved out at age fifteen, Lisi first felt abandoned and then felt the need to liberate herself psychologically from Hans's influence.

I did talk to Hans's older half sister, Erna, who had been a baby when the Gestapo took Rosa away. Erna is eleven years older than Hans and had lived with him only when he was very young. A heavy-set woman with a contagious high-pitched laugh, she is also not speaking to Hans, apparently because of a handful of old and somewhat petty disagreements.

We met in Erna's antiques store in Vienna. There was something Dickensian about the scene, the crowded room overflowing with knickknacks—including a ceramic sculpture of a shepherdess leading a small flock—old murky mirrors leaning against the walls, and Erna in a large beaded necklace giggling in her ornate chair in the corner.

I asked her how she would describe Hans's personality.

"I haven't seen him in many years," she said, breaking into a long laugh. "What I can say is that he is rich in emotions and ideas and that when he has an idea and he thinks this is right, he does it 120 percent. He loves his children and his friends. And he is a very interesting part of all discussions if you have not too many of your own ideas." Erna laughed. "His weakness is to be not too tolerant. He maybe tries to understand, but he cannot hold his emotions. His emotions are overflowing what the brain can control."

In the evenings I would stop in to see Hans and Christine. We would play cards and board games with whichever son happened to be around, then I would go over to Irene's place to watch German MTV and eat mini-croissants with chocolate.

I began to have strange dreams at night: In one I am walking with Hans and the sheep through the West Bank when a suicide bomber explodes nearby, killing a number of people. Hans sits on the ground in shock and asks me if I can continue. In another I am on the run from the Nazis, and for some reason I am careful to take a giant potato with me. In yet another I am on a cruise ship. A fraternity boy on board has somehow died by bringing a pan of onions into the shower with him, and I am being blamed in what turns out to be a classic Jewish blood libel.

I told Hans about this dream one afternoon, and he told me that he had recently dreamed that he was together in a room with all his old girlfriends—all of them wearing beautiful gowns.

# Twenty-nine

# Yiddish Folk
# in Finland

"You have to hear this song," Yukka told Hans.

Hans was on an organic farm in Finland. Yukka was a Sami, a nomadic people from the northern tip of the Scandinavian Peninsula.

"Listen close," Yukka said. "It's a Jewish song but it sounds German, so maybe you will understand some of the words that I can't."

Yukka picked up his piano accordian and began to play "Tsen Brider," a Yiddish folk song he had learned on a farm in Sweden, from a German man. The German man had just come across a copy of a new LP by Zupfgeigenhansel, a West German folk duo. The record was a collection of old Yiddish folk songs titled *Jiddische Lieder*, and Yukka had been so excited by the songs that he copied down all the lyrics and taught himself to play a few.

Yukka sang and Hans listened.

"When I heard these songs, it felt like . . ." Hans made a whooshing sound and held his hand to his forehead. "It struck me down completely," he said. "I was all my life singing, and I had never heard one Yiddish song, at least not that I was conscious of. It was the first time in my life I heard the word 'oy.' "

After telling me this, Hans proceeded through *Jiddische Lieder*, singing a few lines from every track.

"I cannot explain how these songs resonated in myself," Hans said. "I did not even understand many of the words then. But when German speakers listen to Yiddish music, it makes very strange feelings for us. Many words we understand but cannot translate. We feel, if you want, what they should mean. And for me these songs were like a postcard from a sunken world. Maybe in your city you have this culture, but here no one had thought about Yiddish for thirty years."

Hans wasn't the only one discovering Yiddish music at the time. *Jiddische Lieder* turned out to be just the beginning of a blossoming Jewish music scene in Europe. As Ruth Ellen Gruber observes in *Virtually Jewish*, the record was released in 1979, the same year the American miniseries *Holocaust* was broadcast in Germany. The miniseries brought the gruesome details of the Nazis' crimes into millions of German homes for the first time and sparked a new wave of questioning. *Jiddische Lieder* overtly played off of this newfound interest in the Holocaust. The LP came with a booklet that included not only the lyrics to the songs, but also photos and short historical tidbits on East European Jewry.

By the time *Jiddische Lieder* became a hit in Europe, the Jewish music revival had already taken hold in North America. But in America and Canada most of the performers and audience members had been Jewish, a new generation of Jews who were seeking a connection to the world of their parents and grandparents. In Europe most of the performers and almost all of the audience members were Gentiles (there are three separate musical groups with the word "goyim" in their name), and their feelings about the music—especially in the early years of the trend, but still today—have been largely intertwined with their feelings about Nazism. The fad even caught on in Austria. Although Hans is one of the few Austrians to take Yiddish music into the countryside, and certainly the only Yiddish singer to show slides of sheep during his performances, there are at least four other professional groups and performers who play Jewish music in Austria.

Hans had a special connection to the music because his father is Jewish. But I also got the sense after listening to him talk about those first days of Yiddish singing that he sometimes sees himself as just another European leftist who had stumbled onto Yiddish music. After all, Yiddish would have been a perfect fit for Hans even if he had not been half Jewish. He was already interested in old cultures and folk customs, and the music carried with it the victim status that resonates so deeply with Hans. And then there was the fact that Hans is capable of feeling the guilt of German speakers, his leftist, Jewish roots notwithstanding.

"Maybe I could have discovered this music if I did not have Jewish background," Hans told me. "But as my father

is Jew, it makes something special. My father was not interested in being Jewish or talking Yiddish, but I think he still
passed to me some of this *Yiddishḵeit*. He refuses this, but
look how he taught me everything already from when I was
so little. I think this interest in learning comes from being
Jewish. Even if you are not religious, these patterns can affect
the way you look at the world—even how we speak and how
we use our hands and how we go up with the voice when we
want to make a point. And so when I sing Yiddish songs, I
hear back how my father talks, and I try to bring more of this
kind of talking to the songs."

From Finland, Hans went back to Germany to visit his
friends at Finkhof. To his amazement, they already knew all
the songs from *Jiddische Lieder* and could even play some of
them on the guitar. For the next few weeks Hans went on a
Yiddish folksinging binge, learning the words to all the songs
on the record and singing them with every Finkhof shepherd
he could flag down for a duet. It was the start of an obsession
that would leave Hans searching out Yiddish music everywhere he went and memorizing the songs almost as though
he had a duty to do so. Hans soon memorized more than
100 Yiddish songs. But there was still one problem. Even in
Yiddish it was a struggle for Hans to pronounce the word
"Jew."

# Thirty

# Naked in the Alps

Lying on the couch with Irene in the morning, two days before I was scheduled to leave the country, I suggested that maybe I could change my ticket so that we could spend some more time together after I returned from Israel.

"Yes, but what good would that do?" Irene said. "So we'd grow more close for a few days and then you'd leave and it would be even worse."

She was right. I let it drop.

I got dressed and took a train to visit Sepp, an old friend of Hans's who lived in Amstetten. For several years in the mid-1990s, Sepp and his wife had invited Hans's family to live in their basement while the sheep were in the region, and I was hoping he would be able to give me a better sense of the Breuers' daily lives.

On the way there, I sat next to a blond, clean-cut Austrian teenager who could have been a model for a Nazi propaganda poster. We struck up a conversation, and he told me that he was from Ybbs and that both of his grandfathers had fought in the *Wehrmacht* (the German armed forces) during World War II. One had his right arm permanently paralyzed; the other died years later of complications from his war injuries. "When my grandmother talks about the war and how she had to hide her food from the Russian soldiers, she cries," he said.

I asked him how he felt about his grandparents having fought on the side of the Nazis.

"Well, they didn't know what was going on during the war," he said. "They didn't know about the concentration camps and the one and a half million Jews the Nazis killed."

"It was six million."

"Really, six million?"

"Yes, six million," I said. "Are there any Jews in Ybbs now?"

"No, I don't think so. I've never met a Jew."

"Were there any Jews in your town before the war?"

"I don't think so." He paused. "Are you Jewish?"

"Yes."

"So now I've met a Jew." He smiled.

And then something strange happened. I started to feel guilty. Part of me wanted to educate this kid about the crimes of the *Wehrmacht*, but another part of me didn't want him to feel bad about his own family. "I'm not here to point fingers at every Austrian," I lied. "I know not everyone was guilty. I just want to make sense of it."

"Well, the economic times were bad, and then Hitler came and offered people jobs. . . ."

Maybe it was because he was young, but I couldn't get mad at him. Like Irene, he had clearly grown up with an incomplete, if not false, story about what had happened, but he hadn't been able to see through the half-truths. It was hard to blame him for the failures of his Austrian education.

~~~~~

Sepp had a thin beard and looked like a taller version of Bob Dylan. He picked me up in a beat-up Volkswagen Beetle that had no front seat on the passenger's side. As we drove from the train station to his home, he offered to make a detour to see a Jewish cemetery nearby in Ybbs—the town the boy on the train was from. There had been Jews in the area after all.

The cemetery was on a small plot of overgrown grass and weeds enclosed by a low, black-stained concrete wall. The hundred or so tombstones, engraved in German and Hebrew, ran in two straight rows down the center of the plot. Some of the stones were in excellent shape, having been restored, Sepp informed me, by a group of students in the area. Others had faded so that the names were no longer legible.

Along the edges of the cemetery, among the bushes, were a few toppled tombstones. I crouched down and tried to lift one of them, to at least stand it against a tree, but it was too heavy. I've never been a big crier, but something about those tombstones in the grass got me. I fought back my tears. Beyond the wall, I could see fields of yellowing crops and the rolling green hills, spotted here and there with red roofs. The sad little cemetery amid so much beauty felt like a mistake.

I went around and put pebbles at the foot of every tombstone. It took a while, but I found a stone for them all: David Adler, Joseph Brod, Rosalie Brod, Regine Shultz. . . . Most of the years of death were from the nineteenth and early twentieth centuries, and the last year I could find was 1937.

It was hot and silent and strangely still. Sepp watched me from the entrance.

Before we left, we stopped in at the small building that was adjacent to the cemetery. An elderly couple and a younger woman sat playing cards beneath a shelf of Christian knickknacks.

With Sepp as my translator, I asked if any of the families of the dead ever came to the cemetery. The old woman said that there was one family that had come a few times over the years. *The Jewish dead before 1938 were also victims of the Nazis*, I thought. There was no one left to look after them.

Later in the afternoon Sepp and I sat down at the wooden table in his kitchen. I had intended to ask him about Hans, but we ended up talking about Nazis instead. After being unemployed for five years, Sepp's grandfather had taken a job as a carpenter at the Mauthausen concentration camp. He never spoke a word about what he had witnessed until about a year before he died, at which point he began to tell nightmarish stories: He remembered seeing two friends forced to strangle a third friend by standing on opposite ends of a steel bar placed across his neck; he saw a naked prisoner's face pressed into a pool of urine in the ice, then left there for all to see, his nose frozen to the ground.

I told Sepp about the boy on the train, about how he said his family had not known what was happening to Jews.

Sepp said that in the nearby town of Melk, there had been an outpost of the Mauthausen camp. The prisoners were herded in wagons through the city every morning on the way to the surrounding hills, where they were forced to work on tunneling projects and often buried alive. "Everyone would have seen them going through the city," Sepp said. "And even if they did not, they would have known because it's impossible to burn five thousand bodies, as they did there, without anyone being aware of it."

Sepp wasn't surprised the boy on the train didn't know any of this. In 1974 he and several other students had gone through Melk and asked people who would have been between the ages of twenty and forty during the war what they knew about the concentration camp outpost that had been in their city. Almost 80 percent had completely denied any knowledge of it.

Even if the residents of the region had somehow not noticed the smells or had missed the wagons full of Jews, there had been other opportunities to take note of what the Nazis were doing. In 1944, after the Nazis occupied Hungary, tens of thousands of Hungarian Jews were sent to Austria in several different deportation waves. They served as slaves among the Austrian populace, harvesting fields in Styria, digging trenches in the Lower Danube area, and working in factories in Vienna, where they were employed by the city municipality. Many of these Hungarian Jews were literally worked to death. As the war neared its end, an order came in the spring of 1945 for the slave laborers to be marched to the Mauthausen and Gunskirchen concentration camps. The guards, some of them from the Hitler Youth, had orders to shoot the Jews who were too weak to walk. The marches from Styria to Mauthausen followed almost the same path Hans travels with his sheep in the spring. On April 10, 1945, 1,000 to 1,200 Jews walked through Judenburg on the way to their deaths.

I spent the night in Sepp's basement under a LEGALIZE IT marijuana poster, and in the morning I took the train back to Vienna to meet up with Hans and Wolfi. It was the last day I was scheduled to be in Austria, and we were going to drive together back to the flock to pick up several lambs that Hans would then deliver to a Turkish family in Krems.

Along the way, as the mountains of Styria swallowed us up, I told Hans about the conversations I had had with Sepp and Irene and the boy on the train, about how everyone seemed to have a personal link to the Nazis.

"There are thousands of stories like this in Austria," Hans said. "In the first generation you could say not everyone was involved because some people were in other countries and some were really not participating in the crimes. But what happens with the second generation? If a young guy in the sixties had only one relative who was involved, or it was not even his family who was involved, but the father of his bride, still he had to face his father-in-law when he was drunk and speaking proudly of these things he did in Poland. It spreads out with each generation, so that I think now in this third generation we have hardly one family in Austria that is not connected. It is like this rot that the sheep get on their feet. First one sheep will get this disease, and then there can be rot on all the feet in the flock. And if you get these horrible lies about the Nazis when you are young— even if you reject it—also you get parts of it in you. You get these psychological burdens.

"I think the only way to break these things is to at least speak about all the suffering of the victims openly but then also to speak openly about the criminals and the suffering of their families. These criminals were fathers and sons, and this was enormous pain for the women and children they left behind. The psychological key to open the door would be to make groups and to feel this suffering together—not to cover it up, but to say we see all this evil, all this suffering, and don't want to repeat it."

An hour or so later Hans pulled up in front of an old stone building, saying that he wanted to show me the museum his friend kept in the basement. No one answered the door when we arrived, so we walked around to the side of the building, where we encountered a muscular naked man with springy red hair and a leaf plastered across his nose asleep in the grass.

Hans called to the man, and he stood up without seeming the least bit startled that the three of us had just appeared on his property and interrupted his naked nap. Hans explained that we would like a quick tour of the museum. The man happily agreed, put on a pair of black socks and clogs, and led us into his basement museum sans shirt, pants, or underwear.

The museum was called "The Other Homeland" and was dedicated to exposing the ways in which the Austrian fascists and Nazis had used Alpine imagery in their ideological campaign against Jews and foreigners. The basement that housed the museum had once been used as a prison for captured Russian soldiers, and our guide had uncovered some of the markings they had made on the walls.

The first thing I noticed as we entered the cool, damp basement was a large black-and-white photo of skeletally thin children, presumably in a concentration camp, framed by rusted scythes. A pair of boots stuffed with hay stood mysteriously in the corner.

Hans observed from my fidgeting that I was surprised to find myself being led through an exhibit on Austrian fascism by a naked man with a leaf on his nose.

He smiled. "You should take photo of him."

"I don't think that's a good idea," I whispered.

"No, no," Hans said. "I think he would like it."

I took the photo.

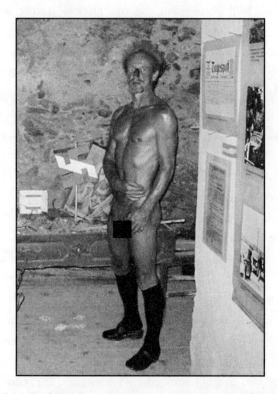

Before we left, the man gave me a magazine he had produced on the exhibit. Inside was a copy of a legal declaration from 1938 stating that Jews within the district of the Salzburg Police Administration were "forbidden to wear any (authentic or inauthentic) traditional costumes such as *Lederhosen*, *Joppen* [traditional jackets], *Dirndls*, long white stockings, Tyrolean hats, etc. Contravention will be punished with fines

of up to 133 Reichsmarks (200 Schillings) or detention of up
to two weeks."

The vision struck me as soon as Hans finished translating: *I ask our guide if he happens to have a pair of lederhosen and perhaps a* Joppe, *some stockings, and one of those
pointy green hats with a feather in it. He says yes, and ten
minutes later I am not walking but strutting through the
Alpine countryside à la John Travolta in the first scene of*
Saturday Night Fever. *Unlike Travolta, I am actually
singing "Stayin' Alive" in my best Bee Gees voice. Soon a
crowd of locals is gaping. I continue to strut, arms swinging,
fingers cupped.*

I think that it was only after I had this vision, which
comes back to me fairly often, that I began to understand
why Hans walked the countryside singing in Yiddish.

From the museum, we met up with the flock. Kati and Andi
were leading the sheep along the edge of an open road. On a
hill above them, a lone horse with a thick white mane gal-
loped back and forth. I watched as Hans said something to
Kati and then scrambled after a good-sized lamb.

I wanted to say good-bye to the sheep, but I couldn't figure out an appropriate way to do so. Also, they seemed busy
with their eating, and I hated to interrupt. I waved at them
through the window of the van and then briefly felt like an
idiot.

On the drive to the home of the Turkish family, Hans
and I got into a long argument over whether there was any-

thing unusual about our tour guide hanging around in the nude. Hans maintained that I was taken aback by the nudity only because I was an American unaccustomed to European ways. "Fine," I said, "but you can't tell me it's typical, even in Europe, for someone to give naked museum tours."

"Yes, yes, it izzz," Hans said, entirely serious.

Laughing, I gave up and told Hans that I was surprised he delivered his lambs across the country rather than just selling them to a butcher.

"I am very proud that we sell directly to the consumer," he said. "This is very important point for me. All our economic system is working in the other direction, and this makes alienation. I want that my clients are getting to be my friends so that we can exchange ideas and eat and perhaps sing some songs together. I do not want to sell my meat to fascists."

We dropped off the lamb to a grateful Turkish man, then returned to Vienna. At an intersection in the city, Hans pointed to a large apartment building. "That was where the hotel was where they tortured my mother and grandfather," he said.

⌒

I was flying to Israel the next morning. I'd see Hans again when I came back for my one-night stopover, but Irene would be out of town the day I was scheduled to be back.

I went over to her apartment to say good-bye and spend one last night with her. We both intuited that it would better not to talk about the fact that there was a good chance we'd never see each other again. Irene took out an undecorated lighter and a bucket filled with silicon tubes and asked me what my favorite colors were.

While my lighter dried, Irene showed me a pair of underpants her friend had made. The friend was an artist, and after discovering that her grandfather had been a big-time Nazi, she had begun to make and sell brown underpants with his photo and Nazi ID number on them. On top of the photo she had written *Opi* (an affectionate term for "grandfather") and dotted the *i* with a heart.

# Thirty-one

# A Flock of His Own

The two women who had visited Hans at Finkhof returned to Krems and brought the idea of Hans leading sheep along overgrown riverbanks in the area before the city council. The city officials were intrigued, since previously they had had to go to the trouble of burning off most of the growth that the sheep would now be dining on. Hans was given permission to bring a flock of sheep over for one year. No money would be exchanged.

And so Hans had a pasture. The next step was to find some sheep. He approached a sheep farmer his mother knew and made him an offer. For fifty schillings per month per sheep, he would take care of the farmer's flock and supply it with all the food it needed. The farmer happily agreed. Hans bought a beat-up old Ford van and began to build portable wooden fences. A friend from Germany arrived to help him start out. Hans still had no home, not even a caravan. Some nights he slept in the van. Other nights he drove back to Vienna and stayed with friends.

Not long after he started the flock, Hans took a bold step. After hearing about another farmer who was interested in having Hans care for his sheep, he briefly tried to care for two flocks at once, driving back and forth from one set of sheep to the other. Everyone told Hans it was crazy, and Hans knew they were right, but it turned out to be an important career move. The first farmer who let Hans care for his sheep changed his mind and took his animals back, worried that the sheep would lose weight in the winter. Without the second flock, Hans would have been a shepherd with no sheep.

But the second flock came with its own problem: The owner of the flock had no money. Hans agreed to be paid in sheep, and after six months he had earned six ewes. A year later the farmer went bankrupt and offered to sell Hans the entire flock for 70,000 schillings before the bank took over his property. Hans had no money. He borrowed from friends and took out a loan. He was in debt and had nowhere to sleep, but with a flock of his own, he felt rich.

# Thirty-two

# Clinging

In 1893, Henry Meige, a French doctor, published a short monograph arguing that the legend of the Wandering Jew had its origins in an actual nervous condition that afflicts Jews. These Jews are wandering, Meige concludes, because they are always in search of the new medical treatments for their imagined illnesses. Meige includes a number of case studies in his monograph (complete with photographs). "Almost all of these Israelites are chronic neurotics," Meige observes, "enumerating their pains and dwelling obsessively on the reading of notes about sensations which they have carefully analyzed and recorded: tenacious headaches, digestive problems, persistent insomnia, erratic aches of the limbs or back, etc."

Later that night, after Irene and I had snuggled and fallen asleep in each other's arms, I awakened convinced that I had AIDS. It made no sense—Irene and I had always been safe—but I was sure of it, just as I had been the time the homeless guy on the subway with the cut on his hand had given me an unsolicited high five or the time I had taken a mud bath and then found out, to my horror, that they don't change the mud between bathers.

And so the trip was ending where it had begun, with me fearing for my life, with me making a mockery of all the very real life-and-death stories I had come to write about. I lay in bed and looked at the white ceiling and hated myself.

But maybe, I thought, there was one redeeming aspect of my hypochondria. Maybe in an odd way, it was itself a testament to the profound evil of the Nazis. After all, hypochondria at its core is a desperate clinging to life, and how better to understand the horror of murder than through the burning longing to be alive—not to be happy or successful or in love, but just to go on for one more day. This is what the Nazis did, I realized. They took all that clinging to life and they gassed it.

When the alarm clock went off at 7:00, I kissed Irene on the forehead and said, "I have to leave. Go back to sleep." My hypochondria was instantly displaced by the misery of separation. *I can't go*, I thought. *This is too hard.* Then I climbed down from the loft and got ready to go.

Irene accompanied me to the Westbanhof train station, where I could catch a bus to the airport. At the station we took photos together in a booth that produced twenty mini-stickers of our faces.

I said, "I know this has all been sort of sudden, but you mean a lot to me."

She said, "You'll forget about me soon," and poked me on the chest.

# Thirty-three

# This Pain!

$B$ack at Christine's apartment a week later, I apologized to Hans for having been unable to find any elderly Yiddish speakers to sing into my tape recorder. I had found something else for Hans: a limited-edition book of songs of his favorite Yiddish musician, Mordecai Gebirtig. Hans was thrilled with the book and immediately sat down on Christine's bed to look through it.

Mordecai Gebirtig, killed by the Nazis in 1942, is one of the most popular Yiddish poets and songwriters, and there is no one Hans admires more. If Gebirtig's story weren't true, Hans would have had to have made it up: Gebirtig lived in Kraków, Poland, where he worked as a carpenter. In his spare time he would write Yiddish songs into the notebooks used by Polish schoolchildren and sing them for his three daughters. He had no formal musical training but had taught himself to play the shepherd's flute. The tender songs he wrote about Jewish life, about the working poor, and later about the destruction of European Jewry he was witnessing spread to Yiddish-speaking communities across the world, but Gebirtig remained a poor carpenter.

As Gebirtig was being evacuated from Kraków's Jewish ghetto along with the other Jews, he was shot in the head by a Nazi guard. It remains a mystery why Gebirtig was shot during the solemn march to the train station while the others were taken away to the Belzec death camp. According to one account from a survivor, Gebirtig was singled out for immediate death because he had suddenly begun to dance and sing in Yiddish at the top of his lungs, as if he had gone mad.

Hans began flipping through the book until he had found "Avreml der Marvicher" ("Avreml the Swindler"), a song about a Jewish street hustler from a broken home. Hans loves the song because it reminds him of the reformatory runaways he tried to help when he was in Spartakus. He particularly likes a line about the poor showing more generosity to Avreml than the rich. "This is one of the crossroads of my shepherding and singing," Hans said. "Often when I am with my sheep, it is only the poor farmers who will help me and give me good food to eat."

Hans then broke into "Avreml," which ends with these stanzas:

> I am Avreml, they call me the swindler,
> In wheeling and dealing I'm always the winner,
> When yet a young lad, to prison I was sent,
>
> I came out a menace with a rare talent, oy, oy,
> I don't hang out in the market with the fellow,
> No, I lie in wait, the filthy rich to collar.

I love gentle people, kind glance and all that,
I am Avreml, quite a winning guy.

Not for long can my story go on,
Broken, ailing, from years in prison,
Just one little hope I still have in my heart—
When death comes and I'm no more driven,
Upon my tombstone let there be written,
With the biggest letters made from gold:

Here lies Avreml, they call him the swindler,
A man of renown, always a winner,
A very fine man, with heart, with feelings,
A pure-souled man, a lone wolf against his will, oy, oy,
Who never did know a mother's love and caring,
Who never did choose the street for his upbringing,
Who never a child nor a father did have,
Here lies Avreml, that winning guy.

Hans ended with a Hasidic melody of *da da da dies*. Christine and I clapped.

"Some sing this as happy song on stage, but I never make this a joke," Hans said, sounding as though he might break into tears at any moment. "Gebirtig did not mean it as a joke. He saw this poor guy in the streets of Poland."

Hans then sang "Motele," a song about a thirteen-year-old boy who defends his own wildness in the face of his father's criticism, just as Hans himself at that age had argued with his father about his radical politics. I liked it both because Motele, the diminutive of Motel, is my father's Yiddish name and because Hans sang the boy's dialogue in a comically high voice to convey his youthfulness.

The last song Hans sang was "S'tut Vey" ("This Pain"):

This pain!
This terrible pain!
Not because of hatred
In the enemy's breast
Nor even the beatings
At the enemy's hands,
Not the Star of David
On our armbands.
The shame!
On all the land
The shame!
On them for all time.

This pain!
This terrible pain!
When it's not the invaders,
Not they!
But Poland's sons and daughters,
Whose own land will rebuke
And turn from dismay.
Gleeful, they poke fun, with laughter
At what they see—
Jews, harried and mocked
By our common enemy.

When Hans finished the song, he read the words aloud in English. And then the tears came, zigzagging silently down his cheeks as he sat atop Christine's bed.

Thirty-four

# To the Mountains

During the winter of 1992, Hans had a vision. For reasons he can't explain, he predicted that it was going to be an especially dry summer, and he became obsessed with finding an area with good grass during the hottest months. If northern Austria dried up, Hans would have to buy hay, which he couldn't afford—the flock eats its own value in hay in three months, and Hans and Kati had always earned just enough to live on. Hans decided that the only hope was to head to the higher altitudes, where the mountain grass would be plentiful even if there was a drought below. He began to call friends, who in turn called other friends, until someone contacted Manfred, who agreed to let the sheep come for a summer stay on the Alpine pasture he had rented that year.

Of course, it turned out to be an especially dry year, so

that by June the grass began to turn yellow, then brown, then dark brown. It was catastrophic for the farmers in the area, but the Breuers and the sheep were already trekking to their hidden green treasure in the mountains.

The change was about more than fresh grass. It was also a chance for Hans and Kati to break out of old patterns of fighting and frustration they had found themselves in. Hans met Kati in 1982, two years after starting work as a shepherd in Krems. Kati was seventeen and Hans was twenty-eight. Because he was much older, Hans was the dominant figure in the relationship in those early years. He taught Kati how to handle the flock until she became an expert herself, training the dogs and building fences as quickly as any shepherd Hans had ever seen.

By 1987, Hans and Kati had two children, whom they would sometimes carry on their backs for entire days as they led the sheep and sometimes hang on trees in woolpacks. They worked as regional as opposed to wandering shepherds in the general vicinity of Krems. Hans fixed up an old abandoned house, and they moved in together. To make ends meet, Hans sheared sheep on the side, coming home in the evenings plastered in wool and hay.

This should have been the point at which Hans's story turned happy. After a tumultuous youth, he had found the job of his dreams and settled down—in his own way—with a wife and children. But happiness has never come naturally to Hans. He loved his work and his sons, but his relationship with Kati was rarely stable. As Kati grew older and more independent, the differences in their personalities became increasingly hard to overcome. Hans wanted to work and intellectualize their problems all day and then have sex at

night. Kati wanted to work equally hard but talk and have
sex less. With Kati's rejections lingering over him, Hans
would find himself once again searching for a sense of security he had never known and once again lashing out when he
couldn't find it.

The problems in the relationship only intensified when
the shepherding became stressful. After spending years on
the outskirts of Krems during the winter, Hans and Kati al-
tered their winter route, taking the sheep through the region's
sloping vineyards instead. The change was the result of a
happy accident. One winter night the sheep had broken out
of their fence and made their way onto a nearby vineyard.
Hans was terrified that he was going to be bankrupt after re-
imbursing the farmers for their crops, but when he approached the flock, he saw that the sheep weren't interested
in the grapeless vines but were instead eating the grasses and
cereals that had been planted between the rows of crops. The
cereals were an ideal protein-rich food for the sheep, and
after proving to the farmers that the sheep wouldn't damage
the crops in the winter, Hans and Kati were given permission to lead the flock across the vineyards. Hans thought he
had struck gold in these barren, snow-covered fields, land
that would have seemed useless to just about everyone else in
the world during winter. But the vineyards were aligned, one
next to the other, making it impossible to skip over a plot of
land where the sheep weren't welcome. And while most of
the farmers thought the flock's presence in winter was good
for their crops, a handful didn't particularly like the sight of a
man in a giant hat crisscrossing their property with his wife,
sons, and 600 sheep. Sometimes the fights with these farmers
got so bad that the police had to be called.

When things got really bad and it felt like everyone—Kati, the farmers, sometimes his sons too—was against him, Hans would retreat into his music, singing to himself and the sheep in Yiddish. The tranquillity of the folk life depicted in the songs about shoemakers and tailors and weddings was eluding him. Hans had become a shepherd, but it hadn't solved his problems.

But in the mid-1990s, as Hans and Kati grew into their new roles as wandering shepherd and shepherdess, the relationship began to improve. Walking with the sheep, the boys at the back of the flock, they would go over and over Hans's emotional problems, trying to understand the link between his outbursts of aggression and his insecurities. It didn't matter so much how they explained Hans's behavior. It mattered that for the first time in years they were talking and working peacefully with the sheep instead of arguing. Hans, who had spent years worrying that Kati would leave him, finally felt reassured.

And then, at least in Hans's telling, Kati grew distant again a few years later. Hans's frustration multiplied as his sexual needs were being left unmet. Kati told him that if he needed sex so badly, he should go find other women to sleep with. Hans thought about it and took her up on the offer. Meanwhile, Kati began spending more and more time playing foosball with the dentist at a bar not far from where their caravan was parked. Hans was terrified, with good reason it turned out, that Kati was going to leave him. Before deciding to travel to North America, where I would meet him for the first time, Hans had begged Kati not to give up on their relationship while he was gone. He returned to Austria to find that his worst fears had come true. His own dentist!

# Thirty-five

# Very Rare and Special

With only a half hour before I had to head back to the air-port, I realized that I had failed to buy gifts for my friends. I ran to the store, and when I returned minutes later with five gum-filled watches, Christine said that someone named Daniela had called and left a number. I couldn't think of a Daniela in Austria that I knew and decided there wasn't enough time to call. But as I was putting the silicon-covered lighter Irene had given me into my bag, I realized that Daniela was Dani, Irene's roommate. I figured I must have left something at the apartment and that she was calling since Irene was in Italy.

"I just got a text message from Irene," Dani said when I phoned. "She'll be home from Italy in a few days. She wants you to stay in Austria and wait for her."

I didn't know what to do. When I had offered to stay weeks before, I hadn't really thought it through. And I wasn't even sure if I could still change my plane ticket. I told Hans and Christine about the new development and then continued to frantically stuff my things into my backpack as the pros and cons raced through my head. Pros: I'd get to spend more time with Irene and finish some of the reporting I had left undone. Cons: I'd grow more attached to Irene, which would just make the separation more painful; money was running low; my AIDS test would have to be delayed.

Just as I was hitting full panic mode, Hans brought over the Mordecai Gebirtig book and asked me to write a note in it. When I gave the book back, he was sitting at the table eating a banana.

"You know what I think?" he said.

"What?" I said.

"I think you should stay," Hans said. "The love of a woman is very rare and special."

I thought about this for a moment. Hans knew what he was talking about. I had come to Austria because I wanted to learn about sheep and Yiddish music and anti-Semitism, but maybe, I thought, this is what I'd take away most from knowing Hans: The love of a woman is very rare and special. Hans meant lovers, but I couldn't help but think of mothers too.

I decided to stay.

Irene wouldn't be back for three more days; in the meantime, I had some unfinished business to attend to. I was going to go back to Carinthia, back to the heart of Haider country.

# Thirty-six

# Searching for Anti-Semites

The next morning I drove to Carinthia with Jürgen, one of
the no-racism.net administrators I met on the same evening I
met Irene. Jürgen was thirty years old and stocky. He had
dark wavy hair, a long straight nose, and a swallowed laugh
that was usually accompanied by a nodding of the head. He
was unemployed, and when I asked him if he wanted to
travel with me and serve as my translator, he said, "Why not,
it's not like I'm doing something else right now," then shook
quietly with laughter.

My plan was to finally find and talk to the Freedom
Party supporters everyone had been telling me about. I had
met the guy at Hans's concert who was against reparations,
and the ignorant boy on the train, but I hadn't yet met anyone other than Sichiovsky who openly endorsed the Freedom

Party or the current government. Carinthia, where 42 percent of the 1999 regional vote had gone to the Freedom Party, was the obvious place to look.

Jürgen stopped at a gas station just after crossing the border into Carinthia. I took my notebook in with me. "Let's do it," I said without irony.

We stood at a Formica counter and sipped Melanges that came with small glasses of water and pieces of chocolate on the side—just like in the Viennese cafés. "How about him?" I said, gesturing toward a mustached man sitting alone in the corner. Jürgen approached the man and repeated the pitch we had gone over in the car: "My friend is a journalist from America. He is writing about his travels in Austria and would like to talk to you in order to better understand the Austrian character."

The mustached man turned to look at me—untucked neon blue polo shirt with big '70s-style collar, hair frizzing this way and that, overstuffed wallet bulging from pants pocket—and shook his head. Jürgen shrugged and tried someone else. Another rejection and then another.

It looked bleak, but I wasn't ready to give up. I bought a big red and white baseball cap that said AUSTRIA across the front. Jürgen couldn't look at me without laughing, but when we approached our next victim, a stern-looking elderly man with exceptionally hairy forearms, he agreed to speak with us.

The man was eating a bowl of soup. I asked him his favorite thing about Austria, and he put down his spoon and said, "Skiing." I asked for his least favorite, and he said, "All the political fighting." He didn't smile and he didn't seem willing to respond in more than two sentences. "Yes," he supported this government and the Freedom Party, and "No," there was not a lot of anti-Semitism or racism in Carinthia.

"But when you think about this government, does it make you question whether Austria has adequately addressed its past with respect to World War II?"

"Austria must look to the future," he said, pausing for a spoonful of soup. "Of course what happened to the Jews is horrible."

Back in the car I found myself disappointed that the old man had not said something nastier. It took me a moment to realize how profoundly idiotic that was—being upset because someone didn't dislike Jews enough. If only he had called me a "dirty Jew." If only he had put down his soupspoon and attacked; or better yet, dumped the soup on my head, shouted *"Heil* Hitler," and goose-stepped out of the gas station with his right arm extended.

There was no more escaping the paradox that lay just beneath the surface of my entire Austrian escapade. I *wanted* the Austrians to be anti-Semitic, wanted them to be every bit as awful as the goyim Bashy had spent so many years warning me about. Not in the past, but in the present. Even a willful ignorance of their countrymen's past crimes would not do. I wanted seething Jew hatred, red-hot and stupid.

It may just have been the frustration of unmet expectations. I had been anticipating my encounters with the Carinthians for months, patiently waiting for the dramatic moment when I would come face-to-face with real evil. A quiet man eating soup in a gas station had not been a part of my vision. But I think my perverse longing for anti-Semites was about something larger. I think it was about the very way

I'd come to understand myself as a Jew. I've always found lots of things to like about Judaism: the acknowledgment that we need a break from the world every seven days, the hyper-ethical Talmudic dictates, the mysterious sense of comfort that comes from the refusal to eat the same delicious foods my ancestors refused to eat. But there is also another side of my attachment to Judaism that I'm less proud of: the side that clings to Jewishness not as an identity to be celebrated in and of itself, but as a response to Jew haters; the side that forgets that to be Jewish is to be more than anti-anti-Jewish. I try to overcome these reactionary tendencies, but that summer I had become so obsessed with the phenomenon of Jewish persecution that the prospect of not finding anti-Semitism in the great anti-Semitic heartland felt, somehow, like a threat to my sense of self. At the time all I understood was that I wanted to find the Jew-hating bastards, but now I see that as Jürgen and I sped toward the heart of Jörg Haider's capital, I needed the anti-Semites as much as they needed me.

We arrived in Klagenfurt and parked in front of the Minimundus—a collection of models of famous buildings from different countries. Jürgen and I took turns peering at the miniature world through a hole in the fence and then stood in silence for a moment.

"Now what?" Jürgen asked.

I didn't know. How exactly do you find anti-Semites? If only there was someone standing on the side of a road selling maps to the homes of the biggest Jew haters.

We walked to the center of town and stopped before a

statue of a winged dragon. I looked into the open mouth of
the dragon, and then I took off my red and white AUSTRIA
hat and pulled out the black yarmulke I had found in my suit
pocket.

"I'm going to walk through Klagenfurt with my yarmulke
on," I told Jürgen.

"Oh, okay," Jürgen said, taking out a cigarette.

I put the yarmulke on and asked Jürgen to trail me from
behind so that he could record the responses I missed. I
walked through the central square and then along the shops
on Klagenfurt's main drag. I lounged on a bench. I stood up
and sat back down and even adjusted the yarmulke on my
head a few times for effect. And yet not one person, not one
single citizen of Klagenfurt, made an obvious show of interest in the circle of black cloth on my head. That's when I realized that I had become the absurd character from my
imagination, the masturbator on the train, the guy singing
with Hans through the night. Fact had caught up to fiction.
It was a shameful performance, and I apologized to Jürgen
for forcing him to participate.

*If only I'd brought a big black hat and a fake beard,* I
thought.

Jürgen and I ate fish in Krumpendorf, the town where
Haider had famously praised the character of SS men at the
annual gathering of Waffen-SS veterans. We put our feet up
on chairs and sipped our coffees in the Mediterranean
breeze. Jürgen told me that his grandfather had been an ille-
gal Austrian Nazi, meaning that he had been a part of the

party even before the Germans arrived. I thought of what Hans had said about everyone in the country being connected to the crimes. Jürgen thought it was probably inevitable that his knowledge of Austria's past had played a role in his political formation, but he wasn't ready to draw a one-to-one conclusion. "I'd like to think that I'd be concerned for human rights even if Austria did not have this past," he said.

At a bar down the street, I struck up a conversation with a drummer in a jazz band. He had long dark hair and was extremely drunk. "I hate that many, many people don't know about our Nazi history," he told me, slurring every other word. "I'm not talking about the old people. The old Nazis will die—fuck you, kiss my ass idiots. But I see young people, fourteen and fifteen years old, and they have their own uniform and they are screaming '*Heil* Hitler' and not knowing what they are talking about. I go to them and say, 'Funny uniform, why are you wearing it?' They say, 'We have to fight for our ideals.'"

Before we left, he asked if I was Jewish. When I said yes, he told me that I looked like Seinfeld and pointed to his nose.

The next day, my AUSTRIA hat back on, Jürgen and I found close to a dozen willing conversationalists at a café in the little town of Moosburg. A jovial man with thick jowls told me both that what happened to the Jews was terrible and that Carinthia's bad reputation was the work of international Jewish organizations. A painter with piercing blue eyes told me that too many minorities in Austria think they deserve special rights and don't understand that they have to assimilate. A bearded handyman in a hat that said

CARINTHIA pointed out that it's not fair that only Austria is asked to look at its past when so many other countries shared in the guilt. A middle-aged woman, who said she supported the Green Party, compared Austria's Nazi years to what Israel is doing to the Palestinians. "It's amazing that they didn't learn from what happened sixty years ago," she said.

Confronted with questions about their country's Nazi past and the need for Austrians to address it, the Carinthians' answers were generally some version of the line I had already heard from the hairy-armed man in the gas station: "Terrible things happened, but Austria must look to the future." Almost everyone we spoke with said they supported the People's Party–Freedom Party coalition government because it was time for a change or because the previous government was not looking out for their interests.

I wouldn't be surprised if any of the Carinthians I met that morning made an occasional nasty aside about Jews. But much as I wanted to be, I didn't feel like I was in the presence of hard-core anti-Semites. If anything, they seemed more xenophobic in their listing of concerns about immigration than anti-Semitic. Even the man who had blamed Jewish organizations for Austria's reputation didn't strike me as being full of hatred. Nor did I get the sense that the people I spoke with supported the Freedom Party because they thought Haider was an anti-Semite or a Nazi sympathizer.

But how, then, could they go to the polls and cast a vote for Haider's party? There were clearly some genuine Nazis around, but the real phenomenon, I began to think, was not that so many Austrians were still vicious anti-Semites, but that the Nazi background of the Freedom Party officials didn't repel them, didn't cause them to cringe with shame or

264 • Schlepping Through the Alps

outrage. They said they thought what happened during World War II was "terrible," and I believe that they believed it. Perhaps it was a sign of progress? The old line had always been that "Austria was Hitler's first victim." Now there seemed to be a quiet acknowledgment that Austrians too had played a role. But as I heard the "terrible" line over and over, I couldn't help but notice how casually the sentiment came out, almost like a rehearsed line. It's possible that some of the indignation was lost in the translation, but I got the distinct sense that the "terrible"s I kept hearing were intellectual rather than emotional "terrible"s. If these people really understood for one minute of their lives how truly terrible the Nazis were, I thought, Haider and the Freedom Party would be impossible.

～

Later that afternoon I took a train to the Styrian city of Graz and met up with Andrea, a friend of Christine's who had offered to show me around southern Styria and to translate my interviews when necessary. Andrea was a tall, forty-four-year-old schoolteacher with a long face and straight brown hair streaked with gray. She wore a hooded rainbow parka and spoke English extremely quickly and with the formality of someone who had been educated in a Victorian boarding school. She seemed kind and yet was so full of nervous energy that I felt myself tensing up whenever she spoke, as though she were my own schoolteacher about to discipline me.

We visited Graz's newly restored synagogue, then headed to Andrea's home just across the border from Slovenia. No longer mesmerized by Austria's mountains, I focused on the shocking number of roadside signs that included the word "schnitzel."

We stopped for dinner in a restaurant where the waitresses wore dirndls. Earlier that year Andrea had organized a ceremony at her school in honor of the rededication of the Graz synagogue. Hans had sung at the event. I asked how she had become involved with the project.

"I am a very passionate Christian, and the roots of Christianity are Jewish," Andrea said, sitting with back erect and speaking at full speed. "So just as you esteem your grandfather very much because he is your grandfather, I love Jews because of that and because Jesus Christ was a Jew."

I smiled and ordered a cheese toast. I had already decided that Jew lovers didn't particularly worry me, but then Andrea would not turn out to be your everyday philo-Semite. Instead, she would turn out to be a philo-Semite who was in love, she confessed, with a "terrible anti-Semite."

"It's really a big problem," she said, emitting a loud burst of embarrassed laughter. "I love him. I love him more than I have ever loved a man. He's brilliant and the conductor of many choirs. He is a very good man in many ways."

Andrea told me that her anti-Semitic dreamboat would call her a Jew whenever he was angry with her and that he would sometimes even do so in public. Andrea's response was to tell the anti-Semite that she herself was a Jew and that if he didn't like Jews, he shouldn't visit her anymore. As she explained this to me, Andrea repeatedly referred to herself as a Jew, and I had to clarify whether or not she was in fact Jewish.

"I don't know what percent Jew I am, and that does not matter to me," she said. "I just said this because all of his arguments made no sense. But then when I said it, I could see how it felt to be attacked as a Jew in public. It is terrible."

"So you're not Jewish?"

"Well, I told him that it does not matter that I'm only a false Jew or something. That's not the point. I told him if he didn't like Jews, then he shouldn't befriend me because I am the same."

"But how can you love him if he's such an anti-Semite?"

"Yes, yes, that's the problem. I believe in his nucleus he is okay, but I don't understand it."

Andrea told me that the anti-Semite attended the ceremony she organized to celebrate the Graz synagogue but had walked out before Hans took the stage because he didn't want to hear Yiddish singing.

"I'd like to talk with this man," I said.

Andrea said that she would take me to a mass in the countryside the next morning and that if I'd like, I could meet and speak with the anti-Semite there. "I will translate all the silly things he tells you," Andrea promised.

Andrea's estate, which she had dubbed "Little Canaan," was surrounded by spectacular sloping vineyards. Her two white doves, Salomon and Susi, were sitting peacefully in their cage, but her two donkeys, Sulamith and Margarete, were missing from the stable. Andrea began to pace around anxiously, speaking even more quickly than usual. We found the donkeys hanging out under a tree some twenty yards

away. Andrea hugged them and fed them a snack she referred to as "donkey chocolate."

I slept in the guest room. The rug was covered in cat
hair. I sneezed and rubbed my eyes and made Yiddish-
sounding *chhh* noises with my throat all night. Andrea slept
on her balcony under the stars. In the morning I tried to plug
in the charger to my camera and received a serious electric
shock.

"Ah, yes, I should have told you that I do not touch that
plug unless I first turn off the power," Andrea said.

The mass was also a celebration of a newly restored roadside
chapel in the tiny village of Wuggau. Andrea announced that
on the way there we would pick up the anti-Semite she loved.

268 • *Schlepping Through the Alps*

A few minutes later we stopped in a parking lot. The anti-Semite stood with arms crossed and a look of consternation. He wore a vest over a button-down white shirt and had a line of thin white hair above his lip that looked like a milk mustache.

The anti-Semite climbed into the car, and we drove on for a few more miles. Then it came out with no warning: a long booming "Shhhhhtop!" It was the sort of authoritarian noise only a real fascist could make. Andrea slammed on the brakes. My body flung forward and then back against the car seat. The anti-Semite got out of the car, retrieved a newspaper from a bag hung on a nearby pole, and returned. Ten minutes later another "Shhhhhtop!" and another newspaper.

"Ah, yes, he very much enjoys reading the newspaper," Andrea said cheerfully.

"Any chance I can walk the rest of the way?" I asked.

"But it is much too far," Andrea said.

In the village of Wuggau, roosters ran free. The mass was outdoors beneath a pristine blue sky. The choir sang round after round of beautiful Ave Marias, and an elderly priest in a white robe and tinted glasses ceremoniously fed wafers to the faithful. Then the oversized beer steins came out and the celebration began. Full-bellied men in Alpine attire played folk ditties on the accordion. Children munched on sausages as big as their arms. After downing a few jelly doughnuts, I asked Andrea if we could interview the anti-Semite. The anti-Semite said he would join us in ten minutes. In the meantime, Andrea pulled aside a thick-boned elderly woman. When I worked my way to my World War II questions, she described how she had lain flat on her back in the vineyards when the Russian soldiers had come through the region. She said that in 1938 her father had warned, "They cheer now, but afterward they will weep." Before walking off, she told me to *"ess, ess"* (eat, eat)—an order I hadn't heard since Bashy used to bark it at me after school every day. If Bashy was here with me, I thought, she and I would be the ones lying on our backs in the vineyards.

By now twenty minutes had passed, and the anti-Semite still hadn't left his table. I was getting anxious that he had changed his mind. I walked over and brandished my tape recorder. He appeared to nod his consent but then made no move to get up. Ten minutes later he stood up and walked in the opposite direction to speak with someone else. After another ten minutes it became clear that he was doing his best to avoid me. Andrea finally dragged him over to a bench with the two of us, but by the time I took out my notebook and tape recorder, the anti-Semite was already up again and walking over to a hunched old man.

"He says you absolutely must interview this elderly gentleman," Andrea said.

"But I want to interview him," I said.

"He says he will do this later," Andrea said. And then the anti-Semite was gone. The old man was a farmer and an organ player. He told me that he had thirty-six cows and that he admired Haider for his intelligence. "Anti-Semitism had always existed since Christ, and I think it still exists," he said. "I think there is now only a little anti-Semitism, but I am afraid it gets worse, because when the Jews get too strong and have too much influence, the people get angry."

"Do you think the Jews have too much influence now?" I asked.

"I don't know," he said. "It's what is reported in the media. Personally, I think we need Jews because even in the former days, if there is no Jew, there is no business. A society can't function without Jews."

I wasn't leaving without my interview with the anti-Semite. It was no longer about what he actually had to say, but about the battle of wills to get him to sit down.

I wandered around until I found him singing in a circle with three other men. I put my hands on my hips and tapped my foot, and when the song ended, the anti-Semite walked back to the bench with me.

# Thirty-seven

# Meet the Anti-Semite

"Tell me your favorite thing about Austria," I said to the anti-Semite. Andrea sat between us on the bench.

The anti-Semite turned to Andrea and she translated. "He says that he will not speak in English because it's the language of Americans and Israel."

I pointed out that English is not, in fact, the language of Israel.

"Yes, but America is a supporter of Israel," he said.

I rolled my eyes. I had wanted it and now I was getting it. The anti-Semite told me his favorite thing about Austria was "the Austrian mentality." "The Austrians are a modest and praying people," he said.

"And your least favorite thing?"

Ten-second pause. In the distance a commotion began to form around the new chapel. The anti-Semite looked downward, his face twisted in thought. He stroked his chin.

"There is nothing that I dislike about Austria," he said. "I like my homeland so much that I can't help but love all the people here."

"Does that include the immigrants and Austrian Jews?"

Thirty-second pause. I began to wonder if the anti-Semite would continue at all.

"I like the way Austrians encounter non-Austrians."

"Yes, but I am asking you about Austrians citizens who are Jews and immigrants. Do you love those Austrians too?"

Fifteen-second pause. More stroking of the chin. "Self-evidently."

An announcement came over a speaker, and then the bell atop the new chapel was rung for the first time. Everyone cheered.

"Is there a lot of anti-Semitism in Austria?"

Twenty-second pause. I looked to Andrea and she shrugged. "It is very difficult how we handle this word 'anti-Semitism,'" the anti-Semite said. "Considering the actual situation between Israel and Palestine, I don't understand the word anymore. Peace would be easily constructed if Israel would retreat from the occupied areas."

"I'm not asking about Israel. I'm asking about Jews in Austria who have nothing to do with Israel."

"Yes, but you can't divide the Austrian Jews from Israeli Jews. By these politics of Sharon, the old anti-Semitism is revived."

"So you think all Jews are the same and have the same political opinion and the same ideas?"

Five-second pause. "Certainly not."

"So the only Jews you don't like are those who support the Sharon government?"

Audible sigh. Twenty-second pause. "The whole world is ashamed by the politics of Sharon."

More ringing of the bell and more cheering.

"Maybe there is a misunderstanding. My question is whether you have any problems with Jews who don't support the Sharon government, considering you just said yourself that not all Jews are of the same opinion."

"If you look at these people here, nobody knows who is Christian, who is Jewish. For me all men are equal whether they are Jews, Muslims, Incas, Christians, or Saudi Arabians."

"So the Jew who doesn't support Sharon is the same to you as any other Austrian?"

"But the Jews support Sharon."

I was beginning to feel like a character in an existentialist play. I was ready to give up. Andrea stepped in and rescued me. "Can I ask you," she said to the anti-Semite, "when you shout at me and call me a Jew, what do you mean by that?"

"I say this because the Jews always feel better than others as the chosen people," the anti-Semite said. "Two times for four weeks in my life I worked in Jewish cemetery in Berlin as a volunteer, and the Jews of Berlin treated the volunteer group very badly."

The anti-Semite was now barking as much as speaking. Amid the hard German sounds I didn't understand was the unmistakable *Juden* pronounced like two words: "You! Den!"

"How many Jews did you meet?" I asked.

"Maybe thirty or forty."

"And all of these thirty or forty Jews treated you badly?"

I never got an answer to that question. The anti-Semite

took off on a rant that brought to mind footage I'd seen of Mussolini giving a speech. His fist came down on his own knee and out came "You! Den!" several times along with several rounds of "*absolut, absolut arro-gant!*"

Andrea translated the tirade as a listing of the anti-Semite's complaints about the arrogant Jews of Berlin. The first time he went, the volunteers weren't given enough to eat. The second time, the Berlin Jewish community had not found a place for them to stay, so the volunteers had to take a long bus trip to and from the cemetery each day.

"So if a handful of Austrians are rude to me, is it fair for me to assume from there that the Austrians are rude people?"

"I worked fifteen summers of my life for social projects all over Europe, and never was I treated so poorly."

"But you would agree that you shouldn't judge a whole community by a few?"

"Yes."

"Okay, so then you shouldn't be saying that all Jews are arrogant, but rather that the Jews you met and worked with in Berlin were arrogant."

The anti-Semite nodded.

"I just can't understand how in this country people can make such haphazard anti-Semitic comments," I said. "Don't you think it's dangerous to say these types of things? Isn't it one of the lessons of the Nazis that violence can start with language?"

Loud sigh. "I just can't understand what Sharon does. What is your opinion?"

"I'm happy to answer that, but first I'd like you to answer

my question. Isn't it dangerous, especially in this country, to make anti-Jewish comments?"

"But this is just restaurant talk."

I started to respond, but the anti-Semite cut me off. "I think that I've learned something from this interview," he said, "and I will consider changing my attitude."

Now I was the silent one. I felt a rush of adrenaline, what I imagine a boxer feels after delivering a knockout punch. Probably the anti-Semite was just trying to shut me up, but for a moment I was able to enjoy the delusion that I had done something important, that I had lowered the overall amount of anti-Semitism in the world. This was what I had been craving all along, I thought: not just for the Austrians to be anti-Semitic, but for the chance to do battle against their anti-Semitism. In fact, my antics over the previous months had almost certainly increased the amount of anti-Semitism in the world. But on that afternoon, in the little village of Wuggau, where the roosters ran free, I had scored one for the Jews.

"I'm happy to hear you will reconsider these things," I said.

The tension evaporated. I think for a split second I even liked the anti-Semite. Andrea referred to me as "Herr Apple," and the anti-Semite said, "Ah, yes, Big Apple," and he laughed.

In the car on the way to the train station, Andrea told me that the anti-Semite would like to see me again the next time I'm in the region.

"Um . . . I . . . yeah," I said.

Thirty-eight

# Wandering Dreams

The Wandering Jew is in Vienna in the 1930s, and, all things considered, he is having a pretty good time. Sometimes anti-Semites chase the Wandering Jew along the Ringstrasse and throw rocks at him, but mostly he is well liked by the Austrians. In the afternoons he goes from café to café, drinking coffee and engrossing himself in the great intellectual debates of the day (the Wandering Jew is a Freudian). At night the Wandering Jew gathers crowds around him and performs magic tricks. For thirty schillings he tells people stories about his travels in strange lands. Usually he makes up the stories because it's hard to remember things that happened 700 years ago.

When 1938 comes along, the Wandering Jew is still making the rounds in Vienna, and with each night, he watches the Viennese grow more drunk on their hatred. Now *as often as not his shows are drowned out by shouts of "Juden raus." Teenagers who had clapped for his magic tricks as young children now yank on the Wandering Jew's long beard and laugh. Old men spit on him.*

*The Jews of Vienna are shocked. They stand before their shattered storefronts and wonder how their neighbors could have turned so vicious. The Wandering Jew knows the Austrians better. He was there in 1348 in Mühldorf [in the archbishopric of Salzburg] when 1,400 Jews were burned alive; there in 1421, when Archduke Albrecht V had the Jews of Vienna who refused baptism burned to death outside of the city walls; there in 1670 to see thousands of Viennese Jews expelled from the city. And some things you don't forget no matter how many years have passed.*

*So when the Nazis come for him, the Wandering Jew is not surprised and makes no effort to resist. He is put on a train and sent to a camp. At night while the other Jews sleep their exhausted sleep, the Wandering Jew walks in circles, round and round, along the edges of the barbed-wire fence.*

*The Nazis don't like all this walking. A young guard takes the Wandering Jew by the arm and drags him into a line of people in front of a concrete building.*

*"You're making a mistake," the Wandering Jew cries out. "I'm the Wandering Jew. The one you've heard about. I can't die."*

*"Into the showers with you, old man," the guard says. The Wandering Jew is stripped of his robe. Naked, he follows the line into the building.*

*The door to the building is closed, and minutes later, when it is opened again, the corpse of the Wandering Jew is dragged out with the others.*

# Thirty-nine

# Dizzy

When I returned to Vienna, Irene was home. We spent the next week traveling to Budapest and going to museums. Hans came into the city the following weekend and met Irene and me at a café. Somehow Hans and Irene ended up singing the Spanish folk song "Gracias a La Vida" together, and when they were done, Irene said it was the most beautiful song she had ever heard.

"I guess you've never heard Yiddish music," Hans said.

We said our good-byes. "I don't know if you will really write a book," Hans said, "but this does not matter. I like having you here." I realized, for the first time, that Hans was onto the fact that I had no idea of what I was doing in Austria. All along he had been humoring me. I gave him an awkward pat on the arm. Then I hugged him.

At around midnight on my last night in Austria, Irene took me to a spa that was part of a communal living project in a building that had once been a coffin factory. Irene was a member of the spa and had her own key. We were the only ones there, and we stripped naked and got into a large bubble-churning hot tub. Irene carried two "noodles"—four-foot Styrofoam sticks—into the tub with us.

"What are those for?" I asked.

"I'll show you," she said. She took one of the noodles, curled it behind my neck, and told me to hold the edges. "Lean back," she said. I did, and she placed the other noodle under my knees so that I was floating naked with my arms spread and knees bent, crucified and crippled. Irene took my feet in her hands and began to pull me around in slow circles. I closed my eyes and listened to the bubbles in my ears. Every few seconds the hot water splashed into my mouth, making me feel as though I was about to drown. I began to imagine I was a captain on a sinking ship, the water about to overtake me. In my head I started to shout out commands to my crew: *Grab whatever food you can! Release the emergency boats!* As I grew dizzy, it began to feel more and more real, almost as though I were hallucinating. It started to scare me and I opened my eyes. Irene was still there, pulling me round and round.

# Postscript

The next summer I went back to Austria to visit Hans and to do a little more research. A few months after this second trip, the political landscape in Austria would change with the Freedom Party suffering a major blow and taking only 10 percent of the vote in the 2002 national elections. The Freedom Party nevertheless held on to its position in the government by again forming a coalition with the conservative People's Party, which saw its share of the vote rise to 42 percent. Shortly after the election results came in, Peter Sichrovsky resigned from the Freedom Party, saying that he had "always thought [Haider] was not an anti-Semite" but that he had changed his mind after Haider's latest round of inflammatory comments. In the state elections of March 2004, the Freedom Party maintained control over Carinthia with 42.5 percent of the vote, a 0.4 percent increase over the party's 1999 total. Haider remains the Carinthian governor.

Austria felt very much the same in the summer of 2002. The mountains were still stunning, and the news was still full of debates about Haider's outrageous antics. And, at least in some respects, I hadn't changed much either. I once again failed to bring appropriate boots or wool socks or a raincoat. But I did bring something much better: my girlfriend, Jennifer.

She was the woman I had been involved with during my senior year of college and then separated from. When I returned from Austria, Jennifer had just moved to New York to work as a lawyer, and on our first date several months later, I felt no moral qualms about my long-term intentions. She had dark blond hair and the softest skin you've ever felt and lips so full and alluring that it required concentration to not impulsively kiss them. When we weren't working or writing, we'd sit around one of our apartments playing "Would you still be my boyfriend/girlfriend if . . ." I'd ask Jennifer if she'd still be my girlfriend if she found out I regularly drank the liquid broth that comes in a jar of gefilte fish. She'd ask me if I'd still be her boyfriend if I discovered she regularly wrote passionate fan letters to Regis Philbin. And on it would go. The answers would usually be "yes," but the answers weren't the point. The point, for me at least, was that I had figured out what was missing from my previous relationships: a shared devotion to the absurd, a shared sense that there was as much fun to be had in imagining as in doing. Only later did I realize that to share a sense of the absurd is also to share a sense of the un-absurd. When the laughter stopped, as it inevitably did, Jennifer and I sat around in Central Park and talked about the pain that some-times simmered beneath the surface of our comic routines. She understood that even as I was joking about my hypo-chondria, I was also not joking. I understood how truly mis-erable it was to be a corporate lawyer.

Irene was also involved with someone else. We met briefly for coffee in Vienna, and I learned she had taken a part-time job as a Web programmer for a Jewish organiza-tion. It was a little awkward for both of us, but it was good to see her after so long. She told me that she had also worked for the Documentation Centre of Austrian Resistance in the last year and had learned much more about Austria's Nazi years. "Now when I ride my bike around the city, I can't help but think about the horrible Nazi that lived in this building or the people who were killed at that building," she said.

Irene asked me if I remembered the song we had sung: *"Hey ho, leistet Widerstand."* I did. We sang it together and laughed at my pronunciation, and then I left.

When Jennifer and I first arrived in Austria in August, Hans was already on the *Alm*. I was anxious to finally see the promised land Hans had raved about—to drink the Alpine milk that he had said tasted like no other milk, to see the rocks he had described as having "soft glowing colors."

The *Alm* was high in the mountains near the Styrian town of Neumarkt in der Steiemark, not far from the Carinthian border. Hans picked us up in the van at the bot-tom of the mountain and drove up a long winding road until we arrived at a sloping green plateau.

"This is the *Alm*," Hans said as I stumbled out of the van, dizzy and nauseous. It was windy and freezing and raining. There was a hunting lodge with green metal shutters and a REININGHAUS BIER sign nailed to the side, and a dilapidated woodshed with a PEPSI-COLA sign nailed to the side. Mohrle gnawed on a lamb carcass next to the door of the woodshed. Christine, Wolfi, a young Turkish couple, and an Israeli woman with her half-Israeli, half-African toddler were waiting for us inside the lodge. (Andi was in Vienna staying in an apartment Hans had rented across the hall from his parents and preparing for the first full school year of his life.) There wasn't much heat in the lodge, and to go to the bathroom, you had to dump a bucket of water in the toilet. Jennifer and I slept on the floor huddled together to stay warm.

During the day, while Hans sang and led the sheep around the mountain, the rest of us worked like Siberian prisoners, hauling heavy stones through the whipping wind and rain to place at the bottom of the fences. At night we were not allowed to leave the lodge because the hunter who owned the property was convinced that even opening a door after 6:30 would scare away his prized chamois. (Apparently, the hunter was monitoring our actions from the base of the mountain with binoculars.)

The Breuers had hauled a foosball table up the mountain, and in the evenings Jennifer and I competed against Wolfi while Hans forced the Turkish man, who played a traditional flute, to learn Yiddish songs with him. The half-Israeli, half-African toddler turned out to be a shockingly precocious cook, and he spent most of his time chopping vegetables with a large kitchen knife. Sometimes the whole group got together to play a card game called Rage.

I was pleased to discover that Hans, if not completely over Kati, was thinking and worrying about her much less often. "I am not happy about what happened with Kati, and I will never be happy about this," he told me, "but I am in less tension with myself now." Kati was still working with the flock, but her schedule had been arranged so that she overlapped with Hans much less often.

Christine told me that after a weekend of working with the sheep together with Hans, Kati, and the dentist, she had decided that she could no longer put up with it and now refused to visit Hans when Kati was around. She had started her own psychoanalysis practice and was shuffling back and forth between her patients and the sheep. Hans told me that they had discussed bringing some of her patients to walk with the flock as therapy.

When I last spoke with Andrea, she told me that the anti-Semite no longer calls her a Jew and that she is no longer in love with him.

～

One afternoon, after Hans had returned with the sheep and led them into the fenced pasture, he announced with a look of real worry that a lamb was missing—he knew because the mother was anxiously calling for her offspring with no response. Hans and I set out in search of the lamb. It was extremely foggy, and I could see only a few paces ahead of me. Hans said that our best chance to find it was to call out so that it might hear us and call back.

We walked together through the clouds, *baaah*ing and *beeeh*ing. Hans found the lamb stuck in a small hole. He wrapped it behind his neck like a wool scarf, and we headed back to the flock together.

"I've never been in fog like this before," I said.

"Sometimes when you have fog like this and you are with the sheep alone, it is like you are in separate universe," Hans said. "It makes incredible impression, so that you cannot imagine how the world continues behind the fog."

# Acknowledgments

Thank you to my agent Jennifer Lyons for making this book possible and for being so supportive, and to Elisabeth Dyssegaard for her invaluable edits and guidance. In addition to the sources I mention in the book, I'm indebted to Professor Anton Pelinka, Heimo Kosjek, Ellen Nickelsberg, Ulf Kintzel, and Michael Schiestl for helping me make sense of my research on both Austria and shepherding. Thank you to Nancy Hernandez, Peter Kanning, Judy Weiss, and Benjamin Sadock for their assistance with translations. A special thank-you to Gerrit Jackson, whose diligent translations of important source material were indispensable. This book would be much worse without the careful reads of Jessica Apple, Talya Fishman, Rebecca Rose Jacobs, Rebecca Phillips, Olivia Gentile, Cuttino Mobley, and David Kaplan. Without the thoughtfulness of Aviva Sufian, who first e-mailed me about Hans, this book would not have happened. Thank you to the students and professors at Columbia University's School of the Arts, especially Lis Harris, for guiding me through the early stages of this process. I'm grateful to Rufus Griscom for his support and for allowing me to maintain a flexible work schedule while I wrote this book, and to Binnie Kirshenbaum and Patty O'Toole for their inspiration. Most of all I'd like to thank my wife, Jennifer Fried, who worked tirelessly to get my manuscript into shape even before we had exchanged our vows.

I'd also like to cite the works that were extremely important to the writing of this book: *Virtually Jewish: Reinventing Jewish Culture in Europe,* by Ruth Ellen Gruber; *Hitler's Austria: Popular Sentiment in the Nazi Era 1938–1945,* by Evan Burr Bukey; *The Covenant of the Wild: Why Animals Chose Domestication,* by Stephen Budiansky; *A Tale of Two Utopias: The Political Journey of the Generation of 1968,* by Paul Berman; "The Passion of Joschka Fischer" by Paul Berman; *Austria: Out of the Shadow of the Past,* by Anton Pelinka; *Guilty Victim: Austria from the Holocaust to Haider,* by Hella Pick; *From Prejudice to Persecution: A History of Austrian Anti-Semitism,* by Bruce F. Pauley; "Herding Dogs Past and Present," by Ann Garner; "Herding Style Is Not a Fashion Statement," by Ann Garner; *Voices of a People: The Story of Yiddish Folksong,* by Ruth Rubin; *The Legend of the Wandering Jew,* by George K. Anderson; *The Wandering Jew: Essays in the Interpretation of a Christian Legend,* edited by Galit Hasan-Rokem and Alan Dundes; *The Haider Phenomenon in Austria,* edited by Ruth Wodak and Anton Pelinka; "The Death Marches of Hungarian Jews Through Austria in the Spring of 1945" by Eleonore Lappin; "War Crimes Trials in Austria" by Winfried R. Garscha and Claudia Kuretsidis-Haider; and *Les Héritiers Contestés: Longo Mai et les Média d'Europe,* by Gilbert-François Caty.

## About the Author

SAM APPLE is a graduate of the creative nonfiction MFA program at Columbia University. Visit the author's website at www.samapple.com.

## About the Type

This book was set in Cheltenham, a typeface created by a distinguished American architect, Bertram Grosvenor Goodhue in 1896 and produced by Ingalls Kimball of the Cheltenham Press in New York in 1902, who suggested that the face be called Cheltenham. It was designed with long ascenders and short descenders as a result of legibility studies indicating that the eye identifies letters by scanning their tops. The Mergenthaler Linotype Company put the typeface on machine in 1906, and Cheltenham has maintained its popularity for almost a century.